The Armour of God

Jimmy Hamilton

Published by

Street Preachers
www.thestreetpreacher.co.uk

ISBN 978-1-911005-21-6

Dedicated to the worldwide
fraternity of street preachers

Foreword

Many a preacher has found in Ephesians 6 a rich vein of truth in Paul's description of the Christian life as that of a soldier. For Paul and his companions, being in a battle was all too real. They had first-hand experience of the hardship, pain, suffering, constant danger and—to use a modern term—friendly fire. All these were part and parcel of the soldier's life, not simply a metaphor. Paul instructs his young companion, Timothy, to *share in suffering as a good soldier of Christ Jesus. No soldier gets entangled in civilian pursuits, since his aim is to please the one who enlisted him.* (2 Timothy 2:3-4). Any glamour or bravado attached to the military life is exposed during the first few days in boot camp. Life there is not a playground but a battlefield.

There is an interesting incident in the history of Israel. The king of the Israel (Ahab) finds himself at war with the neighbouring nation of Syria. Ben-hadad, the Syrian king, boasts of his intention to defeat Ahab. In response, Ahab says: *"Tell him, 'Let not the one who puts on his armour boast like the one who takes it off'"* (1 Kings 20:11).

I have known the author of this book for over 25 years. He speaks with the authority of a veteran who knows the wiles of the devil and qualities to be sought in a Christian soldier. He has been faithful *in season and out* preaching the gospel, not only in the pulpits of our land but out on the streets where the sinners are. I commend this book to you.

Phil Roberts, Stoke-on-Trent

Introduction

The purpose of this book, *The Armour of God,* is to both remind and to challenge Christians that they are in a war. The Lord Jesus warned us of this at the outset of our becoming his disciples (Luke 14:31-33). We ought to be on a war-footing and ever on our guard, equipped to fight and fend off the enemies of our soul and God's church. The tendency is for us to fall in one of two directions. Either we dismiss any thought of supernatural foes; or fall to the other extreme of seeing them behind every trouble in our pilgrimage. The devil, of course, is quite happy to have it either way. It has been said many times before that the best form of defence is to attack. However, I find in my travels that Christians and churches are often ill-prepared to defend the truth, and unwilling to attack the enemy's strongholds. It is nothing short of unbelief. It is incredible! We have quit the field. This ought not to be, and it is time for us to awake from this sleep of death. We are warned of this over and over in the scriptures, that when Jesus comes he will find many unprepared.

It is clear that the poor spiritual climate of the church is no mere local phenomenon. Particularly here in the West It has gone beyond being simply a 'day of small things'. Congregations are diminishing and growing older unless the services offered are akin to a rock 'n roll concert, with all music and very little preaching of God's word. The serious, sharp, evangelistic preaching of the gospel is seldom heard so neither believers nor unbelievers are challenged. There are plenty of PhD's but too little Spirit-empowered preaching that awakens the conscience. Consequently the number of converts to the faith is few. So the growing attitude is, 'Why bother,' either to witness or to preach the gospel. This is to be unfaithful to our calling.

Then there is the opposition we are faced with such as the LGBTQ mafia that has silenced many Christians. Congregations no longer 'dare to be a Daniel' but just go with the flow. The devil is closing us down. We are not just on the back foot. We are surrendering to the enemy, and are unfaithful to the Lord who purchased us with his own blood.

The church must be diligent and steadfast to resist the devil in doctrine and life. How sad is the spectacle of today's church—weak in doctrine, compromising on the truth and decayed with the rot of materialism. The individual cannot successfully resist the devil unless he is a member of a church that is faithful in its battle with sin. The calling of saints is to resist the devil. They must resist his tempting whispers in their consciences and minds, tell him that they hate him and the path he proposes for them to walk and that they will not listen to him. One would think that if the devil is as strong as a lion the saints would be unable to resist him when he attacks. But this is not so, because they have strength from God to do what is humanly impossible. By the Spirit, Samson slew a lion with his bare hands (Judges 14:5-6). We are able to do the same spiritually. We are to resist the devil steadfastly: that is, firmly, strongly and without compromise or hesitation.

Jimmy Hamilton
Newcastle-under-Lyme
May, 2022

Our faith cannot be overcome or destroyed, for Christ has overcome the devil and the wicked world. When we walk in the faith, that is, by the power that faith gives, we are unconquerable. Faith is the victory that overcomes the world (1 John 5:4). When we cling to Christ by faith and rely on the power of our Saviour, we cannot be defeated. (Prof R Hanko)

Finally, my brethren, be strong in the Lord and in the power of his might. (Ephesians 6:10)

A cowardly spirit is beneath the lowest duty of a Christian. You of all men will need courage and determination if you hope to obey your Captain's orders. He commands you, 'Be thou strong and very courageous.' (William Gurnall)

(1)

The Saints' Warfare
(Ephesians 6:10-20)

In the book of Ephesians Paul does what he usually does: first, he lays out the doctrine in the early chapters and then he begins to show his readers the practical implications of that doctrine. He has shown the Ephesian Christians what they are, why they are and how they have become what they are—Christians, that is. The glory of the Christian life has been laid before them. He has spoken to them of God's supreme ability (Ephesians 3:20) and he calls all Christians to live lives befitting their calling. Paul has made it very clear that you cannot live as a Christian until you become a Christian. The word *finally* that commences verse 10 could be translated, *therefore*. Paul often uses this word—because of all that has gone before, here now is the outworking of the matter. And he goes on to tell us of the tremendous power that is arrayed against God, his kingdom and the saints who belong to that kingdom. He calls the saints to live lives worthy of the kingdom (4:1); to maintain the unity within the church (4:3); to grow in maturity and stability (4:14); to deal with anger (4:25f) and impurity (5:3); to be a credible witnesses (5:8); and to be subject to one another (5:22f). You may think, 'Well that's fine Paul; that's sufficient to keep me busy for a while.' Then he comes with this word, *finally*. 'Wait a minute,' he says, 'I'm not finished.

There's something else. To deal with these issues isn't going to be quite as easy as you may think. There are some hindrances. There is your own fallen nature; there is a massively fallen and unregenerate society in which you live; and as if that were not enough,' he says, '*We wrestle not against flesh and blood, but against principalities, against powers, against the rulers of the darkness of this world, against spiritual wickedness in high places* (6:12). And these powers will be working against you, seeking to hinder you from doing the things I've instructed you to do.' 'Just great!' you say. No, Paul tells us, as Jesus himself did, that to be a disciple means entering the mother of all wars (Luke 14:25-33). So, we are told it is also our calling to proclaim and prosecute an irreconcilable war against these forces of evil and powers of darkness. We are not on the defense, but an army marching forward seeking to take the high ground. Thus, we need to learn some of the principles of warfare.

The source of our power for this task is where Paul begins (6:10). He has already given us a clue to this: God's energy, his mighty power (1:19), and the strength of the Lord (3:16). Make no mistake—no one devoid of the Spirit and of the life of God in their souls can accomplish this warfare. The key phrase here is, *in the Lord* (6:10), for it is in union with the Lord Jesus Christ we obtain the strength for the fight. It's a case of being what you are, for as a Christian in union with Christ, you have this constant flow and supply of his power, his might. So, we need ever to be exercising our faith, thus drawing strength for the fight from Jesus. The command to *be strong* is virile; it is akin to a battle cry. The thought is well expressed in the Christian Psalter:

> But of thy pow'r I'll sing aloud;
> at morn thy mercy praise:
> For thou to me my refuge wast,
> and tow'r, in troublous days.

> O God, thou art my strength,
>   I will sing praises unto thee;
> For God is my defence, a God
>   of mercy unto me.
>
> (Scottish Psalter 59:16-17)

It is in the exalted Lamb we have an inexhaustible source of strength and power: *All power is given unto me in heaven and in earth* (Matthew 28:18). It is as if Paul is saying to us as Christians, 'Don't you dare be weaklings, but be strong, in the Lord'. It's a command.

(2)

The Strong Man
(Ephesians 6:10-20)

The Christian is up against a strong foe, *a strong man* (Luke 11:21), but by virtue of the new life that is ours, we have power (2 Timothy 1:7-8). We have a constant supply of all that we need for our Christian lives through our union with Christ. We are united to his operative strength; we are his possession—so his power is our power to draw upon by faith, for he is stronger than all these powers arrayed against us. This is like a sergeant-major barking out the order to his troops, *'Be strong!'* because we need strength and courage for this warfare and it is available to us in Christ. We need this admonition because the seeds of fear that are there in us all need weeding out. The battlefield is no place for souls possessed with fear and discouragement. As an army preparing to go into battle needs to be briefed, so do we. First the logistics, the battle order, the rules of engagement, then the sergeant-major finishes with the rallying cry to his troops, *'Be strong!'* If he finds his army in retreat, then it needs to be stopped and turned around to face the foe again, but then they will need to be even stronger.

Fear is a very contagious thing. I recall reading the history of the American Civil War. There were tremendous acts of courage, bravery and heroism. But there were also tremendous acts of cowardice when entire armies turned and fled the battlefield. Men dropped their weapons, their supplies, food, clothing, ammunition, everything. It only takes one to panic, to turn and run and before you know it everyone else is running too. 'Well,' says Paul, 'We want none of this in this spiritual warfare into which we have been brought. We put on the full armour of God. We don't drop our weapons—our spiritual swords and shields—rather, we stand firm in the Lord. *'Be strong,'* he says, *'Be strong* (6:10), *for the Lord, your God is with you.'* (Isaiah 41:10).

Then, of course, we have the appeals of Scripture to uphold and strengthen us too. We have so many precious promises that we can suck the juice of courage out of. The Bible is littered with them. Think of the picture of the true vine given us by Jesus (John 15:1-11). We are the branches and so we draw all the sap and strength from the vine, enabling us to grow, be strong and fruitful. This is what we need for this battle of the ages: *Say to those who have an anxious heart, 'Be strong; fear not! Behold, your God will come with vengeance, with the recompense of God. He will come and save you.'* (Isaiah 35:4). Think of Joshua, Israel's general, who led them across the Jordan river with the mandate to take the promised land and in so doing to drive out the enemies of God, ungodly, wicked, powerful nations. What is he told as he heads into this warfare? *'Be strong and courageous, for you shall cause* this people *to inherit the land that I swore to their fathers to give them. Only be strong and very courageous, being careful to do according to all the law that Moses my servant commanded you. Do not turn from it to the right hand or to the left, that you may have good success wherever you go. This Book of the Law shall not depart from your mouth, but you shall meditate on it day and* night, *so that you may be careful to do according to all that is written in it. For then you will make your way prosperous and then you will have good success. Have I not commanded you? Be strong and courageous. Do not be frightened and do not be dismayed, for the LORD your God is with you wherever you go.'* (Joshua 1:6-9) That is an Old Testament picture of what we are faced with in these the last of the last days. We're heading for the real promised land, heaven, but on the way there are all these enemies to be conquered. So, we need to be strong as well to obey God's commands, not moving to the left or right and being faithful to our risen Lord in the midst of the fray. This takes more than the world's carnal courage. It takes spiritual, moral courage which we obtain only by spiritual means. Here in these verses, the Holy Spirit gives us our rules of engagement. Alas, we ask ourselves, why is it that there appear to be so few noble-spirited souls willing to stand for the truth?

(3)

The Strength of the Lord
(Ephesians 6:10-20)

Our strength is, *in the Lord and in the power of his might* (6:10), not in ourselves. The Lord, of course, can overcome anything or anyone without us. He does not need us; but without the Strength of Israel (1 Samuel 15:29), we cannot do anything, let alone overcome our foes. We can do nothing of a holy nature and we can obtain no spiritual victory, without the Lord's help. (John 15:5) Concerning the outcome of Christian ministry, Paul asks, *'Who is sufficient for these things?'* (2 Corinthians 2:16). He answers his own question, *'Not that we are sufficient of ourselves to think any thing as of ourselves; but our sufficiency is of God'* (2 Corinthians 3:5). There is a well of grace from which we can fetch strength from the Lord, but it needs fetching, by prayer and supplication (6:18). It is through our conversion by the free, sovereign grace of God that we are in the Lord and consequently, we find ourselves also in the midst of this almighty war. In this we have been promised—and so have access to—his power to preserve us from and to restrain the malice of Satan. He is malicious, hating the Christian with the same hatred that he hates God (1 Peter 5:8). He has a fiendish enmity against the saints of God. He is full of bitter envy at Adam's enjoyment of God and his blessings. If he could have his way, he would treat us as he did Job. He would destroy our families, our livelihoods and our health also. Bless God, Satan is not sovereign; he is not in control. He is on a leash. He is a junkyard dog (Revelation 20:2). God alone is sovereign and he is in complete control. God holds the bridle preventing his evil designs. Satan does only what serves God's ultimate purpose.

We see the strength and power of God working on behalf of his people in his judgments. He smites the ungodly. We see it in Noah's day. As Noah builds the ark the ungodly mock, ridicule and blaspheme, but God takes them away in a flood. They are powerless against the storm of God's wrath. Remember how he dealt with Pharaoh, king of Egypt, smiting him again and again and finally burying him in the Red Sea. The ungodly today continue to speak foolishly against God and treat us with utter contempt. But God, as and when he so pleases, is able to tear them to pieces and cast them into hell forever. God is for us, beloved. He is not against us. We are in a fight, the mother of all fights—but it's a war that has been won. We are fighting a winning battle. So be strong and stand in the power of his might.

We have the strength of his grace, his favour towards us. His strength is engaged on our behalf; it's a matter of faith.

The more you believe, the more you enjoy the strength of the Lord. God loves faith. He loves it when our backs are against the wall and we trust him. He laughs in derision at his and our enemies (Psalm 2:4). Our trust in him brings his strength into operation. *Is anything too hard for the Lord?* (Genesis 18:14). That word *hard* could be translated *wonderful:* 'Is anything too wonderful for the Lord?' The power of grace is not stinted or limited. He is clothed with majesty and divine power—all power. When it comes to your own nature that wars against your soul, there is no passion, no lust, no evil and no temptation that he cannot subdue. There is no misery or danger from which he cannot deliver you. *Now unto him, that is able to do exceeding abundantly above all that we ask or think, according to the power that worketh in us* (Ephesians 3:20). Do you believe that? Take the testimony of the Psalmist. *The Lord is my light and my salvation; whom shall I fear? the Lord is the strength of my life; of whom shall I be afraid? When the wicked, even mine enemies and my foes, came upon me to eat up my flesh, they stumbled and fell.* (Psalm 27:1-2). We watch now in our own day the evolutionary degeneration of Western society, with its return to paganism and the attendant sexual devolution that is its necessary fruit. Will you stand? Will you be faithful? We cannot pitch our tents towards Sodom without ending up with real estate in the place. *'Wherefore come out from among them and be ye separate', saith the Lord, 'and touch not the unclean thing; and I will receive you and will be a Father unto you and ye shall be my sons and daughters', saith the Lord Almighty.* (2 Corinthians 6:17-18) So, *be strong in the Lord, and in the power of his might.* (Ephesians 6:10)

(4)

The Streams of Grace
(Ephesians 6:10-20)

It is only as we act in faith that the streams of God's grace open up to us and supply what we need and that is especially of spiritual warfare (Ephesians 3:14). That prayer is Paul's, but it is inspired by the Holy Spirit. Therefore, it is the Holy Spirit's desire that we are strengthened—and that by the self-same Spirit who indwells us, *for he who is in you is greater than he who is in the world* (1 John 4:4).The Christian man or woman is in the Lord and the Lord is in them. He is the source of our spiritual energy from whom we draw the needed grace and strength to fight the good fight of faith. He who is in the world is the enemy of God and us, his people. He is the cause of the warfare we are having to fight. The Devil's domain is in the earth. He has been cast out of heaven. The apostle John tells us, *the whole world lies in the power of the evil one* (1 John 5:19). The entirety of an unregenerate world is under his sway, his influence. The Devil uses this world of unbelief to rise against the people of God. They are God's enemies and ours. Now you begin to see what we are up against. It is not just flesh and blood—*against principalities, against powers, against the rulers of the darkness of this world, against spiritual wickedness in high places* (Ephesians 6:12)—but flesh and blood too, influenced by these powers of darkness.

But if it is the will of God the Holy Spirit that we are strengthened with his might in the inner man (3:14), what hinders us from being so? Up! About your business, on your knees, for he cares for you. Do you recall in the gospels when Jesus' disciples are in the boat with the Lord? There's a storm and they're petrified. They awaken the sleeping Jesus asking him whether he does not care that they are about to perish.

What does he say to them? 'Where is your faith?' He doesn't say that they haven't got any, but where is it? Where is *your* faith? Are you engaging in this warfare in faith or just letting the enemy ride roughshod all over you? Are you allowing the Devil to scare the living daylights out of you just like the disciples in the storm? *Be not afraid, only believe* (Mark 5:36). *If thou canst believe, all things are possible to him that believeth* (Mark 9:23).

A Christian has no right to be running scared. There is a time when fear must fall away and give place to trust. We are continually with him and he is with us. He holds us by the hand; he guides us with his counsel; and when our time's done takes us up to glory (Psalm 73:23-24). Can we not trust him? Has he ever lied to us? *Casting all your care upon him; for he careth for you* (1Peter 5:7). Yes, in the midst of this anti-Christian warfare, he cares for us. He will not fail us. So, we ought not to be agitated with fear, disturbed by the circumstances and the cares of this world. *He also that received seed among the thorns is he that heareth the word; and the care of this world and the deceitfulness of riches, choke the word and he becometh unfruitful* (Matthew 13:22). We have the victory in Christ. Many enter the field of battle against Satan but few conquer because few have the courage and the resolution to wrestle with the difficulties. Note *we wrestle* (6:12). It is a wrestling match, but it is a fight to the death. Israel comes joyfully out of Egypt but when instead of food and plenty they're faced with war and poverty, they begin to grumble and they want to go back to Egypt. Is that you? Will you turn back and flee in the face of the enemy? Or will you stand and fight? Will you prove the Lord? Will you trust in him and what he has promised? Are you willing to endure hardship for Christ and his cause? Many there are who loathe the idea of losing heaven, but they loathe even more the cost of getting there—the warfare and the fight they find themselves in. They want heaven but at no cost to themselves. They want to get there on the wings of ease, dressed in fine raiment and bellies full. No, it takes another spirit than the spirit of the world to follow Christ fully. It takes the spirit of Caleb. *But my servant Caleb, because he had another spirit with him and hath followed me fully, him will I bring into the land whereinto he went; and his seed shall possess it* (Numbers 14:24).

(5)

The Saints' Armour

(Ephesians 6:10-20)

In order to fight and win this battle, we must put on the Lord Jesus Christ (Romans 13:14). Satan's weaponry will not be deflected by morality, virtue or religion. It is the grace of God and the truth and righteousness revealed in Christ that is needed. A natural man is not fit for this war. He must be born again (John 3:7). We are indeed warned by Jesus against entry into this fray without the necessary resources (Luke 14:25-33). To be without Christ in the war is to be without the armour of God and therefore, you will face defeat. The Christian life is a life of service and warfare. Jesus is more honest than many preachers and churches. In the gospel narratives, he spells out clearly the terms of discipleship and he pulls no punches. If you are to be realistic, victorious, constant and if you're to maintain a clear witness to the light and truth of the gospel, then you have a battle on your hands—the mother of all battles. You are faced not just with the fallen natures of men and the pressures of a godless society, but temptations, snares and assaults from the Devil and his assistants. The war is spiritual and you need armour, God's armour, to be able to stand. You must put it all on (6:11). This is akin to the general commanding his troops: he bellows out before his fellow soldiers, 'Put it on! Put it on!' The picture we're given here is not of a native Red Indian with a bow and arrow. More like a US Navy SEAL all kitted out and heavily armed. I guess Paul would have had a Roman soldier in mind. They were world-conquerors and for a time they ruled it. Each and every piece of the armour is important and is to be put on diligently—the whole array of armour (Isaiah 59:17). This would be over precise for some. It is often the same when we seek to order worship in God's appointed way. Folk want their own self-appointed worship (Isaiah 1:12). Well, this here is what God requires of you if you are to fight and win this war. To correct God's demands is to be righteous over much. If the way and the means are not his we face certain defeat. That which is esteemed by men is an abomination to God (Luke 16:15).

It is God himself who chooses the weapons. Israel in the Old Testament went into battle with horses, against the clear dictate of God's counsel. What happened was a disaster. The horses were houghed (disabled) and the army was defeated. When will we learn it is God's war and we move and we fight under his command? Even the numbers and the weapons were all appointed. The instructions at Jericho were very specific. As they were followed to the letter so victory ensued. Now in the gospel dispensation, we are still at war. We're marching to Zion, the beautiful city of God, heaven. The fighting is intense as we fight against the world, worldly passions and the demonic forces of hell, all arrayed against our souls. God knows and his way is best, always. *If a man also strive for masteries, yet is he not crowned, except he strive lawfully* (2 Timothy 2:5). So, we fight, but we do it in God's way. The defence is not a cover for sin but is to subdue and overcome it. We must beware of a carnal trust in the armour and not God himself. *The weapons of our warfare are not carnal, but mighty through God to the pulling down of strong holds* (2 Corinthians 10:4; 6:10). The ark of the covenant was not God's presence. It was but a symbol of his presence, but it wasn't long before Israel carnally trusted in the ark itself and not God. As long as they had the wooden box they foolishly thought they were protected. The armour is a means, but without God himself, that armour will avail nothing.

(6)

The Saints' Ability
(Ephesians 6:10-20)

The ability of the saints to stand, to be invincible in the face of the enemy, lies here (6:11). The alternative is not just flight, but utter capitulation, ending in a rout. We are to stand as victors in Christ, unvanquished. Therefore, perseverance in the use of the whole armour of God is indispensable. The General's command is, 'Stand!', to be on our guard at all times. The sentry may not fall asleep, nor leave his post until he is relieved. In a war zone, the sentry who does either would face an immediate court-martial and then be shot. And if you are a believer in Christ living in this world you ought not to be asleep (Ephesians 5:14). And neither have you as yet been relieved of your duties (Mark 13:13). God's grace flows to us through the armour, for putting on the full armour of God is the same as putting on the Lord Jesus Christ. Thus, the grace of God comes to us through Christ (Romans 13:14).

We are to pray without ceasing. We pray, but we pray in the Spirit, as without the grace of the Lord we cannot pray as we ought (Zechariah 12:10). Why are our prayer meetings throughout the land today dull, boring, dead even? Because we lack this very thing of which the prophet speaks, *the spirit of grace and of supplication* (6:10). There is no spiritual life without the life-giving Spirit of grace.

In the ongoing battle against the flesh, Paul, in a very real sense, disowns the stirrings of sin as alien intruders to his new life in Christ. *For that which I do I allow not: for what I would, that do I not; but what I hate, that do I. If then I do that which I would not, I consent unto the law that it is good. Now then it is no more I that do it, but sin that dwelleth in me. For I know that in me (that is, in my flesh,) dwelleth no good thing: for to will is present with me; but how to perform that which is good I find not. For the good that I would I do not: but the evil which I would not, that I do. Now if I do that I would not, it is no more I that do it, but sin that dwelleth in me* (Romans 7:15-20). These intruders have no right of entry, Paul has no desire for their interference now that he is a new man. But he has to fight them off. He has to slay them. How? *If ye through the Spirit do mortify the deeds of the body, ye shall live* (Romans 8:13). He says, *evil is present with me* (Romans 7:21). Put the letter 'D' in front of the 'evil' and you have the enemy that Paul has to fight. And so too do we. It is the Devil who stirs up the evil, kindling the fires of sinful thoughts, feelings and desires. Then he stands back and accuses us (Revelation 12:10).

Our forgiveness is real, but Satan does not want us to enjoy that forgiveness. He tempts and he taunts and accuses us. If he can get us preoccupied with our sins and failures or keep us bound to our besetting sin or sins, he will leave us bereft of any enjoyment of God and our new life in Christ. He is ever seeking to destroy our peace and to distract us from serving God. If he can get you in a downward spiral, burdened with feelings of guilt and shame, he knows you will consider yourself totally unfit for service. How he loves to keep you there. If he can blot out all thoughts of Jesus who tells you over and over that you are forgiven—Be *of good cheer; thy sins be forgiven thee* (Matthew 9:2)—Satan will have the upper hand, draining you of the good cheer, the joy of your salvation. Yes, there are times when we have sinned and we need to put it away (1 John 1:7). We need to make restitution if we can, but, we need to resist the Devil. Instead of submitting ourselves to his relentless taunting and accusing, we need to, *submit... to God. Resist the devil and he will flee from you* (James 4:7). That is the answer and we have the God-given ability through the Lord Jesus Christ. Put him on, and *make no provision for the flesh, to fulfil the lusts thereof* (Romans 13:14). To be clothed in Christ is to be clothed in the whole, the full armour of God.

(7)

The Attacks of the Enemy
(Ephesians 6:10-20)

The enemy, Satan, the devil (6:11) *was a murderer from the beginning and abode not in the* truth, *because there is no truth in him. When he speaketh a lie, he speaketh of his own: for he is a liar and the father of it* (John 8:44). He is cunning, crafty, a deceiver. His expertise lies in deception. This is one of the main reasons for his being chained during the New Testament age, to keep him from deceiving the nations (Revelation 20:1-2). He has an army and is no mean commander of his forces. He knows his business. We need to be realistic. Both he and his temptations are real. He must be discerned, resisted and refused on the basis of truth (Matthew 4:4,7, 10; 1 Peter 5:9). He is not beneath using even your best friend to fulfil his purposes (Matthew 16:22). He is filled with rage: *Woe to the inhabiters of the earth and of the sea! for the devil is come down unto you, having great wrath, because he knoweth that he hath but a short time* (Revelation 12:12). Those of course who have fallen asleep at the wheel, spiritually speaking, the complacent, or the backslidden, will know nothing of the battles with the devil. He has them exactly where he wants them to be and they are of no danger to him at all. In fact, it's most probably his doing that they are in that state. Or, if you do truly belong to Christ and are in any one of these spiritually defective conditions, it is possible that he, the devil, may be loosed upon you to awaken you to your perilous position. We must all be resolved to go on with Christ, knowing that we have such a formidable foe to deal with. For this is a battle we will never win on our own or in our own strength. You may say, 'Well, I know nothing of these fights of which you speak, I have never been confronted with the devil. I am at peace; all is well; all is smooth sailing.' Well, could that be because you are travelling in the same direction as he is? Examine yourself (2 Corinthians 13:5). We must face up to him courageously when he attacks but keep him and his filthy dealings in perspective. He is defeated; he has been conquered; he is a junkyard dog; and he is chained and under the control of the sovereign Lord Jesus Christ (Revelation 20:1-2).

He has been comprehensively beaten (Colossians 2:15; Hebrews 2:15; 1 John 3:8). In times when he is attacking us, we need to be calm, stand still and in our minds take hold of the gospel facts. Recognise that Christ has defeated him once for all. This will help us to be *strong in the Lord and in the power of his might* (6:10). Take hold of what we are *in Christ*, what He has made us and understand that *in him* we are strong. Think of how we have been blessed in limitless ways (Ephesians 1:3-8; 2 Peter 1:3-4). We have been raised to new and immortal life. We are or we should be, living on the victory plane (Ephesians 2:4-6). Be strong!

And yet he is cunning; he is crafty; and he is not called the serpent for nothing. He is wily and we must seek to understand his wiles. He can make us think and feel weak. He can make us think that the odds against us are too great and therefore we give up the struggle too soon. This is especially so in terms of our personal victories over sin and our sphere of service. He will tauntingly and powerfully suggest to you that you will never get the victory over a particular sin that you are fighting, or that your service for the Lord is valueless. He will certainly seek to discourage you when it comes to prayer. One thing Satan cannot abide is to see Christians on their knees. Therefore, to make the stand that we are commanded to here, we need the full armour of God on, at all times.

The apostle Paul now begins to show us what that armour is and how we are to put it on and use it. But foremost he would have you to know the enemy and his stratagems that you are up against. He comes in many guises and he may even appear as a minister of the gospel. So we need to be able to recognise him in order to be able to stand against him. We need the tools to out-think this grotesque monster. Our God has provided us with all we need.

(8)

The Wiles of the Devil
(Ephesians 6:11)

We are still in verse 11 where we are told to stand not just against the devil, but his wiles also. He has much experience, is an expert and deception is his primary tool. He leads an army that is at his disposal and is no mean general when it comes to the art of warfare. However, he cares for nothing of the Geneva Convention in his tactics and there are no holds barred. He has many devices and most of these are performed in a sheep's skin. There are some who have been ensnared by him and need to be recovered (2 Timothy 2:26). We, Christians, are warned by the apostle not to be taken captive by him (Colossians 2:8). In his wiles he can take in the wise and the simple, the hypocrite and the upright, the timid and the bold, the rich and the poor, the aged and the young. We need to learn to be discerning. We must be equipped to know the difference between the hissings of Satan and the inspirations of God, so that we can recognize the hook hidden within the bait.

The word *wiles* (6:11), indicates scheming cleverness and craftiness. He appeared to our first parent Eve as a shining one and beguiled her with spiritual talk very appealing to her. He implanted the seed of pride into her (Genesis 3:1-6). He can appear as an angel of light (2 Corinthians 11:14). You will find him in the realms of the aesthetic, the artistic, the intellectual, as well as the gross, the ugly and the perverse. He has his failures, who are to be found in the gutter and are of little further use to him. He is ambitious, so he does not seek a kingdom that consists of human wrecks. His ambitions are higher than that, better, more powerful. He has a lust for power over others that exceeds any. His targets include ministers of the gospel. This is one of the reasons Jesus seeks to quench the notion of popularity amongst his men. He himself walked away from any suggestion of this himself. *When Jesus, therefore, perceived that they would come and take him by force, to make him a king, he departed again into a mountain himself alone* (John 6:15). Do not crave popularity, my friends! It's a curse and, even worse, it's a wile of the Devil. The cunning of the Devil takes some matching for efficiency. He studies situations and personalities and lays snares where you are at your most vulnerable. He often knows the Christian better than the Christian knows himself. He watches for where and when we are on our guard, and waits for a more opportune time when we are careless and tired.

His strategies and activities can be learned by studying some of the Old Testament saints. Take for instance Elijah's suicidal depression; after a mighty victory over the false prophets of Baal, he is found under a tree convinced of the failure of his ministry. He is sure that his ministry is finished.

But the truth is he had already been used tremendously and God yet had more work for him to do. The devil will make black look white to us and white black. The prophet suffered from tiredness and confusion inspired by the Devil. But God cared for his servant. He held him, ministered to him and restored him. The Devil was defeated. He will put poison in a golden cup. He will present you with much profit if only you will yield to sin. He hides from view God's wrath that you would incur and the misery that would be a reality as a result of the sin. Again, with Eve, he offers her the bait but he hides the shame, the holy displeasure and the wrath of God. He hides the loss that follows her by taking the bait. He puts enormous fallacies before men, which he leads them into and leaves them with a fool's paradise. He will promise them prosperity and perhaps even give them such. He will promise them pleasures unlimited; success—if only they will sell their souls to him. Then he will sink them into the deepest hell. Therefore, *put on the whole armour of God, that ye may be able to stand against the wiles of the devil* (6:11). *Be sober, be vigilant; because your adversary the devil, as a roaring lion, walketh about, seeking whom he may devour* (1 Peter 5:8).

(9)

The Ruses and Realms of the Devil
(Ephesians 6:10-20)

Yet another of the Devil's ruses is to confuse people (6:11) and especially so in regard to the character of God, making him out to be hard and unreasonable, a hard taskmaster. He will suggest to you that God's requirements of obedience will most surely frustrate your own aspirations and pleasures. In his wiles he will seek to convince you that obeying God is beneath your human dignity and most certainly your destiny.

How high you could climb and what you could achieve in the world if you weren't hampered by the restrictions of God's word. He will cause you to question and doubt God's word as he did Eve in the garden of Eden. If he can get you to question your dependence upon God and his word, he will soon have you doubting God's good intentions for you. You will find yourself questioning whether God really is for you (Genesis 18:25; Romans 8:31). Before you know it, you are in a state of confusion. This the Devil loves. This is a ruse of the Devil (6:11). He masquerades, causing you to think that he doesn't exist, or he is a music hall joker not to be taken seriously. The two extremes he will take you are either to deny his existence altogether or to see him in absolutely everything that goes wrong. There is no end to his ingenuity. The Bible speaks of false christs (Matthew 24:24); of false apostles (2 Corinthians 11:13); of false epistles (2 Thessalonians 2:2); and of false miracles (Matthew 7:21f). He is the Devil and he is the author of all that is false in the spiritual realm. Not all that is of a spiritual nature is necessarily of God. We must develop and use discernment (1 John 4:1). The Devil is persistent. Maybe you are having a quiet spell and all is peace and quiet. He has left you alone and you think it is wonderful. Be aware, on your guard! He will return. He hasn't gone away or forgotten you. Remember how he tempted the Lord Jesus in the wilderness, again and again. Then we are told he left him, but it was just *for a season* (Luke 4:13). He awaits an opportune time. He is determined, so you must watch and pray. *Watch ye and pray, lest ye enter into temptation. The spirit truly is ready, but the flesh is weak* (Mark 14:38). This is not a time of peace—not yet. We are at war.

His realm is this world's scene and he is wrathful. We should not be surprised at this. He hates and persecutes the church and we are told to expect this. *Therefore rejoice, ye heavens and ye that dwell in them. Woe to the inhabitants of the earth and of the sea! for the devil is come down unto you, having great wrath, because he knoweth that he hath but a short time. And when the dragon saw that he was cast unto the earth, he persecuted the woman which brought forth the man child* (Revelation 12:12-13). He is seeking to establish his own kingdom on earth, the kingdom of man without God (Revelation 13:1-4). His design and determination is to make war against the church. He is operating now (2 Thessalonians 2:7). There is always a sense of mystery regarding the fact and operations of evil, but they and he, are for real.

Be warned, he roams the earth. He uses people in places of power in the state and in the church. If he can influence, control the state and the pulpit, he can control the nation. He takes hold of a Jeroboam and all Israel is steeped in idolatry. He is ever seeking to poison the cistern of the church. If he can infiltrate the Seminary, the Bible College, he can defile the students, who in turn go out and defile the church. If he can get them to cry peace when there is no peace, he has won the day. He uses the 'few' clever ones within the church (1 Corinthians 1:26f). God's kingdom is managed in a godly simplicity. It is wisdom, not so much cleverness, that is needed. This is not to say that the church does not need clever men. Of course she does and we thank God for such gifted folk. But there are dangers of carnal reason instead of biblical reasoning, thinking God's thoughts after him. The Devil is spiritual, demonic, diabolical. He uses foolish leaders too, filling the church's membership role with silly souls that have never been reborn. The church's worship then is altered to the humour of these silly souls. Let us be assured from this passage that the apostle confronts us with that which we are up against—the personal, organised powers of evil (6:12). They are the cause of spiritual blindness in the world, in godless humanism and moral decadence. Evil and the power of evil are facts. The objective reality is that the nation of the church (1 Peter 2:9) is at war. Are you in fighting mode?

(10)

The Rulers and Authorities
(Ephesians 6:10-20)

Our struggle is not simply against flesh and blood, enough though that may be. We have the pressures of a godless society to cope with. We believe in the personality and power of Satan. He is the head of an organised kingdom of evil. I emphasise the word organised. His insidious, deceptive operations must be seen behind those of men, nations and world events. It's not hard to see some of his triumphs in Western society today—the spiritual blindness, the godless humanism and the moral dissolution. The greatest of those are men left with no sense of their eternally derelict state. Evil is a reality. Its power is factual, objective and something outside of ourselves. We are not talking about personality defects. We are talking about personal evil that is not explained in a human, biological, or psychological way. Hence, the spiritual warfare we are engaged in (6:12) is not a clash of human personalities or philosophies, even between belief and unbelief, though these means are used by the dark powers. No, we are against an omnipresent, persistent and sleepless malignity of evil forces. The word of God is clear that this world order is under the sway of the evil one (1 John 5:19; Revelation 12:12). The entire world's ethos is contrary to God and we are urged not to allow ourselves to be seduced by it. *Do not love the world or anything in the world. If anyone loves the world, love for the Father is not in them. For everything in the world– the lust of the flesh, the lust of the eyes and the pride of life– comes not from the Father but from the world. The world and its desires pass away, but whoever does the will of God lives forever* (1 John 2:15-17).

Our patterns and mindsets can so easily be squeezed into the world's mould without us noticing. So, we have to take deliberate countering measures. *Do not conform to the pattern of this world, but be transformed by the renewing of your mind. Then you will be able to test and approve what God's will is–his good, pleasing and perfect will* (Romans 12:2). We need to remind ourselves that the world hasn't just forgotten God. It has rejected him. This is what the apostle Paul means by a spirit of, or attitude of lawlessness (2 Thessalonians 2:3-4; 2 John 7). The world's activity is an organised kingdom of evil with operational agents, both humans and spirits, all actively working against God—and even some who profess an allegiance to God. Their main objective, of course, is not us but Christ, though Satan hates us as he hates Christ. He is intent on disturbing and destroying all who belong to Christ. With his Machiavellian schemes, he will, given the chance, use us to harm God's people and work. Then when we have served his purpose he will cast us off without mercy or reward, just as he did with Judas (Matthew 27:3-4). However, in spite of the complexities and activities of evil, we must keep in mind that he, Satan and his kingdom are already defeated. And so we use the whole armour of God and without fear, we stand.

(11)

The Spiritual Attraction
(Ephesians 6:10-20)

The enemy of God and of our soul works through every department of human life: intellectual, aesthetic, cultural and religious. The development of sin is clearly seen in the 'civilised' world as never before. Satan takes hold of and uses the world's intellectual and scientific capacities. Make no mistake, he makes himself appear attractive, very attractive. He is the master of deception, do not ever forget that. The manifestation of Satan to our first parent Eve was brilliant, dazzling and so very shrewd (Genesis 3:3). He has not changed. There is a hypnotic aura, shine, brilliance to him that enables him to draw hordes after him. Rest assured you are not dealing with that cartoon character with a horn on his head and a pitchfork in his hand. He wields a diabolical power. He is like the Pied Piper, alluring by sight, sound, appearance and desirability. He can captivate a person's mind and in doing so he has them ensnared. If he can condition the minds, the pattern of thinking of men and women, he can increase his kingdom ten-fold. How do you poison a lake? Do you take a bucket of poison and go dump it in the lake? No, you go to the source, the spring, the fountain and you poison that. The stream will do the rest, carrying the poison into the entire lake. How do you poison society? Same way. You go to the fountain—the schools, the colleges, the universities—and poison developing minds. And the poison will be carried out into every part of that society. So where do you think you will find Satan most active? At the spring, the fountainhead of society, in education, in science, in medicine and in politics. The entirety of the lake of society is thus poisoned with the venom of Satan's anti-God thinking. He sows the poisonous seed then sits back while sinful, unregenerate humanity does the rest of the work for him.

The disaster and development of the fall are coming to full fruition today, leading I believe to the consummation of history. We see the development of the kingdom of the Antichrist, the kingdom of man without God. There is promotion of rebellion against God, denials of Christ and utter lawlessness. He has puffed up their minds, deluding them into thinking that there is no limit to what man alone can do, without God. It is the old lie: *Ye shall be as gods* (Genesis 3:5) and, *Go to, let us build us a city and a tower, whose top may reach unto heaven* (Genesis 11:5). His aim is to oust God from his throne by declaring the sovereignty of man. This is the lie he feeds into fallen, rebellious man's mind. You are sovereign, you can rule and you can solve your every problem on your own, without God. His power is evil and it is for real. It is determined wickedness. It is seen in the gospels in the personal experiences of Jesus. You see his wiles working against those who set themselves to obey God. He comes against them with a vengeance. If you are determined to get yourself right with God through Jesus Christ, you are in for trouble, spiritual trouble I mean. There is going to be a battle for your soul make no mistake. He does not lie down easily. He comes with his tormenting accusations, brutal assaults and crafty corruptions against the believing people of God. He is after all the prince of Hell. You better believe it and you better be armed, with the full armour of God (6:12).

(12)

The Spiritual Warning
(Ephesians 6:10-20)

This, our present text, is of great value when faced with people who are ruthless and merciless; those, that is, who are driven by the enemy, Satan and who are determinedly against us as Christians and against the cause of Jesus Christ. Remember, *we do not wrestle against flesh and blood, but against the rulers, against the authorities, against the cosmic powers over this present darkness, against the spiritual forces of evil in the heavenly places* (6:12). If we can discern the tools, instruments and the dupes of Satan it helps; and if we can grasp that all the human ferocity will not stop them it helps; because behind such evil men, there is a spiritual wickedness driving them. With Christian discernment and an understanding of the warfare we've been called into we can learn to cope, to fight and even to conquer through Christ

Jesus our Lord. We don't make excuses for evil and the people who are the perpetrators of it, but perhaps understanding its source can ease the personal hurt and grief that we ourselves may experience because of their deeds. If we begin to realise that evil people are taken captive and even blinded by the enemy—*The god of this world has blinded the minds of the unbelievers, to keep them from seeing the light of the gospel of the glory of Christ, who is the image of God* (2 Corinthians 4:4)—and if we can but remember that we are at war, not simply against flesh and blood (6:12), then these trials take on a clearer perspective.

But we do also wrestle against flesh and blood. There is our own flesh for instance: *But I say, walk by the Spirit and you will not gratify the desires of the flesh. For the desires of the flesh are against the Spirit and the desires of the Spirit are against the flesh, for these are opposed to each other, to keep you from doing the things you want to do* (Galatians 5:16-17); and that of others, that we have to fight against. But over and above the opposition of flesh and blood there is a worldwide network of cosmic powers, spiritual forces of evil at work (6:12).

This conflict extends even beyond the confines of this world. It extends to heavenly places (6:12). Of course, such concepts stretch our minds beyond their limits. We live in a day when there is a lot of unseen activity in what we call outer space. Because this activity is out of sight we seldom give much thought to it but it is there nonetheless. There are satellites circling the earth that provide us with much of the technology we use. We are told they are used by governments to spy on us, watching our every move and monitoring our activities on earth. In fact, some find the development of this technology to be quite scary. It is all, I'm sure, part and parcel of the development of the totalitarian state, the pursuit of man's sovereignty without God. It's all ripening for the coming Antichrist and his short reign (2 Thessalonians 2:3-4; Revelation 13:1-10). However, all of this is not an occasion to fear. The revelation of God's word is given to his people to counter such fear, for the entire kingdom of these cosmic powers and forces of evil have been defeated, overcome and shown clearly to have been so: *He disarmed the rulers and authorities and put them to open shame, by triumphing over them in him* (Colossians 2:15). This was won on the cross. In the death and resurrection of our Lord Jesus, we have the victory. There is absolutely nowhere in all of the scriptures that suggests to us that the throne of God has been disturbed or is even uncertain, let alone assailed or toppled. Our God reigns, supremely, sovereignly! There is no doubt about this: the God of peace rules. Picture if you will as we close this section, what John saw: *I looked and behold, on Mount Zion stood the Lamb and with him 144,000 who had his name and his Father's name written on their forehead* (Revelation 14:1). That is a picture of Jesus, God's Lamb, standing in the midst of the entire church on earth. He is there with his blood-bought people, defending them, fighting for them and dealing with these cosmic powers, the forces of evil. We have the mighty warrior God, our Jesus, on our side and thus we are assured of the victory. Just hold on to Jesus and ride out the storm.

(13)

Galvanised with the Truth
(Ephesians 6:10-20)

The whole armour of God needs to be taken up and utilised in order to render us victorious in this fight (6:13). The apostle now begins to explain to us what the complete armour, piece by piece, begins with the truth (6:14). To galvanise something in engineering terms is to give a piece of iron or steel a protective layer of zinc. It prevents corrosion. So, Paul urges us to take action to prevent the corrosion of our faith, to galvanise ourselves with a layer of truth. In other words, we must act upon the truth revealed to us by God. In an evil day we need the ability to stand (6:13) and it is only by standing upon the truth of Scripture we will be able to do so.

A soldier in the field of battle will only conquer if he is *fully* armed. Seven in Scripture is the number of completeness within the covenant of grace and hence we have seven items that make up the full armour of God: we have truth, righteousness, the gospel of peace, faith, salvation, the word of God and finally prayer. All these are needed for conquest. Here (6:14) we begin with the divine, saving truth, the reality of God's utterances. Paul likens it to a soldier's belt worn when on duty. The Christian soldier is never off duty. We must remember that this warfare is not just about our own personal salvation, growth and well-being, though that is included. It is about the worldwide plan of redemption, the filling up of the kingdom of God's dear Son. It is about the complete and devastating defeat of the cosmic powers and spiritual forces of evil (6:12), so our personal battles and victories are vital because they are all part of that. But sometimes we need to be reminded of the bigger picture. The entire thing is scary unless we remember two things. First, we do not fight this war in our own strength. Second, the final outcome is not uncertain: victory is assured. We must maintain our focus upon the all-sufficient, limitless power of Jesus Christ (Ephesians 1:19; 3:20) and be galvanised with the truth of this.

One of the ways the devil, our enemy, seeks to sidetrack us is by getting us to lose our focus on Christ so we focus overmuch on ourselves, our sins and our failures. Settle your mind on the truth of God's forgiveness. Your sins cannot be greater, or stronger than God himself (Zechariah 3:1-5). Our forgiveness is a reality, truth. The sin-stained prodigal was restored without hesitation and reinstated to the privilege of serving with joy (Luke 15:20f). The truth of God's wonderful and free salvation *must* galvanise us. It is settled and cannot be reversed. This is our justification, God's declaration of the repentant sinner, 'Righteous!'—and none can change that declaration, not even God. He will not go back on his word of truth.

This applies to the big picture too. The kingdoms of this world will be the Lord's. This is his blood-bought world and don't ever forget it. *Then the seventh angel sounded; and there were loud voices in heaven, saying, 'The kingdoms of this world are become the kingdoms of our Lord and of his Christ; and he shall reign for ever and ever'. And the four and twenty elders, which sat before God on their seats, fell upon their faces and worshipped God* (Revelation 11:15-16). Grasp hold of this belt, the truth, and hold fast to it. Galvanise yourself with it. The battle is won or lost in the mind, but the truth of the gospel is unassailable if we but gird our minds with it. *Wherefore gird up the loins of your mind, be sober and hope to the end for the grace that is to be brought unto you at the revelation of Jesus Christ* (1Peter 1:13). To focus on the truth is to daily have our minds renewed with Scripture (Romans 12:2) and to know the truth about our own salvation (Romans 6:3). It is only from the truth of God's word that we will get the assurance, the courage and the confidence to fight and win. It comes from the facts, the truth of God that can be relied upon to the utmost. *There is therefore now no condemnation to them which are in Christ Jesus* (Romans 8:1). *What shall we then say to these things? If God be for us, who can be against us? He that spared not his own Son, but delivered him up for us all, how shall he not with him also freely give us all things* (Romans 8:31-32)?

(14)

The Truth Expressed
Ephesians 6:10-20)

When we speak about the truth in Christian terms we are talking about doctrine and life. One is the dynamic of the other. The truth is the truth of the gospel, the propositions of the word of God which are to be believed in their entirety for salvation. This body of truth is the dynamic of the spiritual and moral life manifest in those who confess our Lord Jesus Christ. The gospel is the truth and it speaks the truth (John 17:17). We will never fully understand the world in which we live—the human race of which we are a part and the reality of its state before God—until we have truly believed the word of God. Otherwise, we will fail to understand man's true state and his great need. Some people complain they need to understand to believe, but this is the wrong way round. We need to believe in order to understand. Else we will be ever searching without finding.

Not only is the truth to be confessed but also falsehood must be renounced (Matthew 23:1ff). The apostle Paul testified to the Ephesian elders how he had kept back nothing of the truth from them but had declared to them the whole counsel of God whilst in their midst (Acts 20:17-21). He declared the same testimony amongst the Thessalonians (1 Thessalonians 2:3ff). We have similar testimony given in the Old Testament regarding expressing the truth with integrity, from the prophet Samuel (1 Samuel 12:1ff). The testimony was also borne by the prophet Daniel (Daniel 6:1ff). Again, the apostle Paul lays before us a very searching passage in 2 Corinthians 4:1ff. In particular, verse two says: *We have renounced disgraceful, underhanded ways. We refuse to practice cunning or to tamper with God's word, but by the open statement of the truth we would commend ourselves to everyone's conscience in the sight of God* (2 Corinthians 4:2). Anything that militated against the service of the gospel was put aside. This is where 'reformation' bites on both the inside and outside of our beings. If the truth has not penetrated the inside and reformed our hearts and lives we face nothing but utter defeat in terms of Christian warfare. Faith with a good conscience is a necessity. God looks upon the heart (1 Samuel 16:7). He desires truth in the inward parts (Psalm 51:6). Faith and good conscience go together. If one is missing we will end up shipwrecked (1 Timothy 1:18f). Our lives must ring true.

If there are any flaws the devil is bound to use them to trip us, not just to shame us (which is bad enough and gives him great pleasure) but to cast a shadow upon the gospel and ultimately upon God's name. If we are going to fight for truth and God, we must be true within. Any deceit, any sin, must go; we must we seek and work to reform the heart and slay all falsehood. The truth must be expressed, but in deed as well as in word.

If our hearts have truly been changed, we will most certainly have a fervency regarding the truth. Some people wonder why preachers get so excited when they are preaching. If the reality of the truth has been grasped, there will certainly be an earnestness, a conviction and without doubt an excitement. If the truth never really thrills us, have we truly believed it—I mean concerning the person and work of Christ and what he has done for us? Do we ever say to one another, 'Isn't it great to be a Christian?' or 'Isn't it great to have the truth proclaimed?' Do we ever actually rejoice together—spiritually, I mean—because of what we have been given, or has our Christian service been reduced to just talking? If you read through the Acts of the Apostles again you will see that is how it was with them: rejoicing, serving one another and reaching out to a lost world. Because the truth had so galvanised them, they themselves had become identified with the truth itself; not just the content, but the dynamic too. As they were carried along by the truth they became preachers of the truth, not in the formal sense, but with lip, life and service they embodied the truth (6:14).

(15)

Armour-plated Righteousness
Ephesians 6:10-20)

The heart needs to be kept, protected: *Keep your heart with all vigilance, for from it flow the springs of life* (Proverbs 4:23). We need the breastplate of righteousness (6:14b). Sin prises open the links of the chainmail, and the cracks expose us to danger, as the lurking enemy is waiting for any opportunity to pounce (1 Peter 5:8). He will seize upon anything that he can use to charge us with wrongdoing, for he is not called the accuser of the brothers for nothing (Revelation 12:10). A fault, whose presence you cannot deny, he will use to torment you night and day. He will plague you with it. It is his delight that such guilt would dominate and spoil your peace and your Christian life. He will disturb your every conscious and waking moment until you are paralysed in regard to any Christian activity and service. Some don't read the Bible because it opens them to his accusations. They are convicted. They no longer pray, attend the meetings, or bear witness to the Saviour: their armour has been breached. The righteousness of Christ must lead to righteous living, else the enemy will cripple you.

This is the very nature of the warfare the Christian is called into. You have been drafted into the King's army, but the warfare is spiritual. It is not like the wars of the world, that can be explained by worldly and historical causes. Our aim is not a natural one. It is not pointed at or desirous of the conquest of some world power. The weapons we use are not physical or material, *for the weapons of our warfare are not of the flesh but have divine power to destroy strongholds* (2 Corinthians 10:4). We fight by the power of faith with the sword of the Spirit, God's word. The battle is the Lord's, not man's. We look to the Lord to supply everything necessary for this fight. This is the reason men are bidden to count the cost of discipleship before they begin. *What king, going out to encounter another king in war, will not sit down first and deliberate whether he is able with ten thousand to meet him who comes against him with twenty thousand? And if not, while the other is yet a great way off, he sends a delegation and asks for terms of peace. So, therefore, anyone of you who does not renounce all that he has cannot be my disciple* (Luke 14:31-33).

So we look to Jesus our Captain, our mighty warrior God (Isaiah 9:6). He refused help in his darkest hour but trusted himself to God, forbidding his men the use of carnal weapons. *Then Jesus said to him, 'Put your sword back into its place. For all who take the sword will perish by the sword. Do you think that I cannot appeal to my Father and he will at once send me more than twelve legions of angels'* (Matthew 26:52-53)? Muhammed's clan of thugs made no progress at all in the sixth century until they started using the sword. Muhammed is termed the prophet of the sword, and still to this day they advance their cause by the sword and terror. The kingdom of God and his Christ are not advanced in this way, but by spiritual means: the prayers of the saints, the teaching of God's word and the power of God's love captivating and drawing men's hearts. The fiercest battle Jesus ever fought was upon the cross. Paradoxical as it may seem compared to the world's wars and Islam's, he conquered in death. He conquered sin and death and hell by his own death. Despite people's misunderstanding, it was the same in the Old Testament too. Israel of old was a type of the church. She was hated by the surrounding nations—that is, the world. Their hatred of Israel was spiritual because she was God's chosen nation. The wars that Israel fought were fought on spiritual terms: *How could one have chased a thousand and two have put ten thousand to flight unless their Rock had sold them and the LORD had given them up* (Deuteronomy 32:30)? In faith they had to look to God for the victory and it was when they failed to trust God, they faced defeat. The New Testament is no different. The battle is between light and darkness (2 Corinthians 6:14). It is a spiritual battle fought in the midst of the world, the family, the school and the workplace as God's people seek to live out the principle of their new birth in Christ in accordance with the word of God. This, the sword of the Spirit, the word of God is our only weapon. Our defence is his righteousness (6:14b).

(16)

The Need of Christ's Righteousness
(Ephesians 6:10-20)

The breastplate is a necessity. It protects our vulnerable heart (Jeremiah 17:9). To be clothed upon with and to stand in the righteousness of Christ is a must. It is this truth that is the foundation and the dynamic of a righteous life—the truth concerning the righteousness of Christ. *'Behold, the days come,' saith the Lord, 'that I will raise unto David a righteous Branch and a King shall reign and prosper and shall execute judgment and justice in the earth. In his days Judah shall be saved and Israel shall dwell safely: and this is his name whereby he shall be called, The Lord our righteousness'* (Jeremiah 23:5-6). It is the righteousness of another that enables us to stand before God uncondemned (Philippians 3:9; 1 Corinthians 1:30). He, Christ, is the source of our life and it is because of him, that we are in him and that we live (Galatians 2:20). It is forensic. We are judged and declared by God to be not just 'not guilty', in his court, but 'righteous altogether', because of another's righteousness—Christ's. This is a central part of God's saving truth. It is this that makes our hearts impenetrable against Satan. God's verdict acquits us of sin and its guilt and declares us righteous. We are naturally related to Adam (Romans 5:12). Because of him we were dead in sin (Ephesians 2:1). We were dead not because we sinned. Rather we sinned because we were born dead, but now in Christ we are alive (Romans 6:3-11). He, Christ, died, was buried and raised from the dead; and we were in him, so we too have been raised to newness of life. All that he has accomplished is ours in him, freely, graciously, as if it were our very own—the forgiveness, the righteousness, the favour, all the blessings of God—ours! (Romans 8:33ff).

Once Adam was our federal head and all that was his, sin included, was ours. But now we have a new covenant head, Christ, and all that is his is now ours, so his righteousness becomes ours. Sadly this is so seldom preached today. The thought that we can be held accountable for Adam's sin is a horrific thought to many. But if we reject the federal headship of Adam, where does that put us regarding the federal headship of Christ? This is our great comfort. Faith declares us to be in Christ (Romans 8:1). Our faith declares that at Calvary all our sins were paid for in full: past, present and future. I was crucified with Christ, raised with Christ. Now I live, because of him. I stand in his perfected righteousness, an armour-plated righteousness that Satan the devil cannot penetrate. This was earned, purchased, not by me but for me, by Christ. The sentence and the pawl of death hovers over the world, but we can shout, 'I LIVE!' So who is your federal head? Is it Adam or is it Christ? It is one or the other. The old spiritual song asks of you, 'Were you there when they crucified my Lord?' The answer is, yes, you were. We were all there, in our Adamic natures, under his covenant headship. Only through faith in Christ, with him as our federal head, clothed upon with his righteousness, are we protected from sin and its consequences, now and in the last day.

(17)

The Need of Personal Righteousness
(Ephesians 6:10-20)

The life of Christ in us is but the beginning. We are, one might say, in the process of being saved through sanctification. If we are not in that process, we are on the pathway to perdition. We still live in the body and it is a body of death as the apostle Paul states in Romans 7:24. The flesh remains, hence his plaintive cry, '*Wretched man that I am! Who will deliver me from this body of death*?' We also face the fact that *the last enemy to be destroyed is death* (1Corinthians 15:26). But it is no longer the doorway to hell, but to the resurrection and to heaven itself. We still sin but the principle of regeneration remains. The principle of grace and holiness is indestructible. It is ours and we are safe for time and for eternity in Jesus—and so we are able to stand (6:14), not in any righteousness of our own, but that of Christ and Christ's alone. Our righteousnesses are as polluted rags: *But we are all as an unclean thing and all our righteousnesses are as filthy rags; and we all do fade as a leaf; and our iniquities, like the wind, have taken us away* (Isaiah 64:6). Were we to attempt to stand against the enemy, Satan, in our own righteousness we would soon be pierced through. We would not be able to stand without the breastplate of Christ's righteousness (6:14). Imagine going into this warfare in our filthy rags (6:12)? Jesus warns those who wish to follow him without understanding this principle of spiritual warfare: '*Or what king, going to make war against another king, sitteth not down first and consulteth whether he be able with ten thousand to meet him that cometh against him with twenty thousand? Or else, while the other is yet a great way off, he sendeth an ambassage and desireth conditions of peace. So likewise, whosoever he be of you that forsaketh not all that he hath, he cannot be my disciple'* (Luke 14:31-33). If we cannot renounce our own righteousness and trust in Christ's alone, we cannot enter this spiritual warfare and expect to win. In fact, Jesus says we cannot be his disciples.

God has made provision, for us, a protection for our hearts against the enemy of our souls—the breastplate of Jesus' righteousness (6:14). By faith we go forth, trusting in what Christ has accomplished on our behalf. This is what the armour of God is for. We can stand unashamedly in the perfect righteousness of Jesus, delivered and relieved of our sense of shame. Our hearts are cleansed.

A right spirit is essential for fruitful gospel service. *Create in me a clean heart, O God; and renew a right spirit within me* (Psalm 51:10). The prophet Isaiah: *And he saw that there was no man and wondered that there was no intercessor: therefore his arm brought salvation unto him; and his righteousness, it sustained him. For he put on righteousness as a breastplate and an helmet of salvation upon his head; and he put on the garments of vengeance for clothing and was clad with zeal as a cloke* (Isaiah 59:16-17). We have been entrusted with a stewardship: the proclamation of the gospel. Therefore, we must be assured by faith that we have been personally credited with the righteousness of God's Son, Jesus Christ, if we are to know the gracious power of God attending our service (1 Thessalonians 1:5). Our hearts are kept safe and warm in relation to God as they are constantly kindled with the love of Jesus. We are willing and confident to fight the spiritual battles, to fight the good fight of faith.

But a warning note in finishing here is appropriate. This letter was addressed in the first instance to the church at

Ephesus, which was very soon to lose its first love: *Nevertheless I have somewhat against thee, because thou hast left thy first love* (Revelation 2:4).

(18)

Shoes for the Feet
(Ephesians 6:18)

As a result of the gospel, you are now filled with gospel peace (Romans 5:1) and are eager to hit the road with the good news to others (Romans 1:15). But before you go you need some shoes on your feet, gospel shoes (6:15). This readiness is not for an invasion, but rather to stand against the schemes of the evil one (6:13), for the forces of hell are—not will be—loosed against you (6:12). So, we need to be prepared to stand and fight, inspired by the gospel, because of the objective peace we have with God through Christ (John 14:27); the gospel that also brings us subjective peace (Philippians 4:7). The wrath of God has subsided and the blood of his Son Jesus has done its propitiating work (1 John 2:2) and now God is with us (Romans 8:31). Now we are prepared for the battle, so let it commence. With the experimental knowledge of the gospel we're good to go. The enemy forces over us are like a swarm of locusts closing in. We have two choices only, to flee before the enemy as chaff in the wind or take hold of the courage instilled in us by the gospel and stand. The readiness that is ours is because the gospel is not only the gospel of peace but also of truth. The peace that is in our hearts reveals itself in our feet. 'How come?' you say. Because we are now ready to carry the good news of the gospel to the world. Every single Christian is called to be a missionary; not necessarily in a full-time capacity or abroad, but on your own doorstep, in your neighbourhood. Wherever you be you should be 0carrying the gospel with you, for we carry with us the assurance that this gospel with its contents is reality: it is truth. If we don't have the belt of truth on we're lost before we start (6:14a). The true gospel is peace and brings courage to our hearts. We have been reconciled to God. Our quarrel with him is over. But it was the truth of the gospel that produced this, nothing else (Romans 3:23f). We ourselves were one time at war with God in our minds and our foolish hearts were darkened (Titus 3:3; Romans 8:7). There was a deep-seated hatred in us against God. But we heard the preaching of the gospel, as God declared his terms of peace. In turn our eyes were opened to the truth as it is in Jesus and the grace that justified us before God (1 Peter 3:18).

The truth has brought peace to our minds. We are reconciled; for Christ has spoken peace to us, has pacified and comforted our hearts and minds. It was to our advantage that he went away (John 16:7) because it was as a result of the fulfilment of his work on earth that this reconciliation is ours. Only on that basis could God the Father apply the terms of peace to us. This peace God sends to us but only on the basis and on account of the death of his beloved Son. This was the means God himself devised that he may be seen to be absolutely just and the justifier of ungodly sinners. God forgives and reconciles, but his justice remains intact. The death penalty has been exacted, not on us, but on Jesus. We go free. Now we are at one with God and with his people too. There can never be peace between the two seeds, the seed of the woman and the seed of the serpent. But by the gospel of peace, we now have a love for and a unity with the people of God (Psalm 133:1f). Only the gospel of truth can so knit people together. This is the powerful effect of the gospel accepted sincerely in faith. Outside of the truth of the gospel, there is only fury, wrath and darkness. It is the gospel of truth that sets us free.

(19)

The gospel of Peace
(Ephesians 6:10-20)

Notice how all the items of armour are correlated, interlocking with each other. There is progression even. We embrace the truth, God declares us righteous and we have peace with God and the peace of God (Romans 5:1; Philippians 4:7).

The apostle here speaks of gospel shoes (6:15), not carpet slippers. We are to be ready to hit the road with the good news of God's salvation to the world's sinners, not ready for bed. We need shoes that we will be able to stand in and be prepared, ready for whatever we meet. We do not want to find ourselves distracted, even disabled by feet that are uncomfortable, for we are in for the long haul, long-term service. We are not engaged in short-term missionary service, you know, just to see if it is suitable for us, or perhaps if the climate suits us. We need to be quietly and inwardly assured of our calling, settled regarding the nature and the outcome of our service for the Lord Jesus Christ. The soldier needs to be sure of his capacity and competence to serve and that his cause is a just and righteous one. It is only then that he will not be easily shifted, standing firm in his gospel shoes, at peace with God and having his mind garrisoned with that peace. A squad of soldiers is an impressive sight and one that discourages trouble-makers. When we as Christian brethren are thus united, as a band of brothers, persuaded of the truth of our message and service to God, we communicate the same impression—a powerful, positive impression. This is not just in defence of God's revelation, but also attacking with it—advancing and pulling down the strongholds of the enemy, assured of the outcome. We are called to engage in the mother of all wars, a spiritual war, against demonic hosts and the wiles of the devil. *For we wrestle not against flesh and blood, but against principalities, against powers, against the rulers of the darkness of this world, against spiritual wickedness in high places* (6:11-12).

But the outcome of the conflict has already been decided. We are on the winning side. We may not be five-star generals, colonels or even sergeants. We may be just squaddies who have landed on the beach and have got to the first sand dune. Our job is to get to the next one and, who knows, maybe we won't make it. Perhaps we'll be killed in action. No matter, it's win-win. We go to heaven anyway. So we fight the fight of faith with this amazing peace in our hearts, this assurance of the final outcome. This peace is positively encouraging because it is grounded in the facts, the historic facts of the gospel.

The war and its outcome are not even our responsibility. We cry with Judah of old, *O our God…we have no might against this great company that cometh against us; neither know we what to do: but our eyes are upon thee* (2 Chronicles 20:12). This is our peace, resting in God in his might. The battle is the Lord's, for his resources are limitless, though invisible. His servants patrol the earth night and day. *I saw by night and behold a man riding upon a red horse and he stood among the myrtle trees that were in the bottom; and behind him were three red horses, speckled and white Then said I, 'O my lord, what are these?' And the angel that talked with me said unto me, 'I will shew thee what these be.' And the man that stood among the myrtle-trees answered and said, 'These are they whom the Lord hath sent to walk to and fro through the earth.' And they answered the angel of the Lord that stood among the* myrtle-trees *and said, 'We have walked to and fro through the earth and, behold, all the earth sitteth still and is at rest'* (Zechariah 1:8-11). So clothed upon with the whole armour of God we are ready and we have the capacity for service that stands on our conviction of the truth revealed to us, the everlasting gospel, our message of peace that will bring peace to others.

(20)

The Grace of Peace
(Ephesians 6:10-20)

Peace is a spiritual and gracious gift of God (Galatians 5:22). It is that grace gift that guards and keeps our hearts immovable in Christ Jesus. *And the peace of God, which passeth all understanding, shall keep your hearts and minds through Christ Jesus* (Philippians 4:7); *Thou wilt keep him in perfect peace, whose mind is stayed on thee: because he trusteth in thee. Trust ye in the LORD for ever: for in the LORD JEHOVAH is everlasting strength* (Isaiah 26:3-4). It is a supernatural peace that is of God and so the devil cannot move us from our gospel stance and Christian practice. The guard spoken of here in Philippians is akin to a sentinel, a soldier on guard duty. God's peace is that soldier guarding and keeping our hearts so we can't be moved from the basis, the foundation of our peace: the gospel. We cannot be kept from expressing the gospel or our worship of God in our daily lives. O the enemy may try, but that's why daily we need to put on the whole armour of God. If our peace goes, we become restless, physically, mentally and emotionally. It is then we begin to drive ourselves, seeking to work more and feeling like we'll never succeed. Then we become tired and weary and sad, driven by the devil and not led by Jesus. We know nothing of the quiet and confidence that the prophet speaks of, *For thus saith the Lord GOD, the Holy One of Israel; 'In returning and rest shall ye be saved; in quietness and in confidence shall be your strength'* (Isaiah 30:15-16). When we get ourselves into trouble and our peace is disturbed the solution is the same as before. It was not our works that got us right with and at peace with God to begin with; It was faith; it was trust. And that is still the answer, to trust, in the gospel.

So, the answer is not our striving, but rather to learn to be still, to cease from our own works and a renewed awareness of God (Psalm 46:10), for he hasn't moved. He is still there, still with you. Did he not promise that? Sometimes we get to running around like headless chickens, almost as though the whole cause of God, including our own salvation, will all collapse if we're not doing. God is in control and we live and work under his orders, so we can rest. We can let the peace of God rule our hearts, letting them return to their rest, to the God of peace, because God will not fail us. He has promised. We have a covenant signed and sealed with the blood of his Son. It is an inviolable and unbreakable covenant. And part of that covenant package is peace: *Peace I leave with you, my peace I give unto you: not as the world giveth, give I unto you. Let not your heart be troubled, neither let it be afraid* (John 14:27). He assures us that he has prepared the way, *And if I go and prepare a place for you, I will come again and receive you unto myself; that where I am, there ye may be also* (John 14:3). It is only when we begin to forget the facts of the gospel that we lose our peace. That peace is a confiding, trusting, in what God has done. If we are not at peace, it is saying we are not trusting, simple. God has given us a good prescription for peace (Philippians 4:4-7, 10-13), but our gospel peace must be thought of in the context of the spiritual warfare and service we have been called up to. The peace is promised in the midst of the battle, not out of it. If you have disengaged yourself from the warfare, sought terms of peace with the enemy, or if you have become a spectator of the battle scene, then no wonder if you have no peace. If you quit the fight or compromise, the devil will give you peace. He'll leave you alone, for sure—but we don't want the devil's peace! We want God's peace, yes?

(21)

The Spiritual Force-field
(Ephesians 6:10-20

The complete, the whole, armour of God is likened to a force field, an energy shield that deflects the assaults of the enemy (6:16). It keeps him from penetrating the citadel of our minds. In all circumstances take up *the* shield of faith (6:16). The definite article I think is needed because the reference is first of all to the objective faith of the believer. The objective is what the subjective embraces. The objective truth of the gospel is what protects us from the blazing, fiery missiles of the devil, his temptations. And that is what they are, *flaming darts* (6:16). Just as Eve when she was tempted to doubt God's word ought to have answered, 'No, I believe God's word.' But she did not and the rest, as we say, is history. We ourselves ought to answer likewise, 'I believe the objective truth of God's word. It is written, therefore I believe.' To hold up the shield is to hold up the word of God, the doctrine of the gospel. The apostle Paul probably has the picture of a Roman soldier's shield as he pens this (6:16). It was thought to have been about four feet in height, something like what our riot police use, covering their entire bodies. If you formed a row of Roman soldiers with their shields up, you would have a virtually impenetrable wall. With this shield, you can withstand the wiles of the devil (6:11), for he is actively and viciously hostile to God. He cannot touch God so he goes for his woman, his bride (Revelation 12:13-17). He furiously pursues her. He fires his flaming darts tipped with the poison of his lies. The power of Satan is in the lie. He is the great deceiver, the father of lies (John 8:44; Revelation 20:3). He seeks to set our minds ablaze with his lies about God and about Christ and the gospel. Think of the fire that he started in Eve's mind which still burns today. The devil is a fire raiser. You get no warning, but he comes at you in different ways, at different times and seldomly the same way twice. His schemes are many (6:11), so we need to be prepared, always clothed upon with the whole armour of God in all kinds of circumstances. It may be temptations, surges of feeling, or something that takes you by surprise that stings you to react. It can be personally or corporately in the church, where he seeks to set a whole host of fires in our midst until the whole church is ablaze.

He may seek to panic us, sowing and growing the seeds of great fear in us. He may set thought patterns in motion, suspicions, criticisms, accusations, or disagreements. We need the shield of faith in all circumstances (6:16). Sometimes we get caught by friendly fire, as also happens in a war zone. It might be a close friend who is feeling ignored for some reason and it may or may not be genuine. The devil seeks all such occasions. His schemes are calculated to bring confusion, distraction, distress and division amongst God's people. Be assured these are not of God, *For God is not the author of confusion, but of peace, as in all churches of the saints* (1 Corinthians 14:33). But he, Satan, has studied us well. He knows where we are vulnerable and how to get the reaction he wants. We need that shield of faith (6:16).

He is a fear raiser too. He will take things from your past, bring them to mind and accuse you. 'What if people knew about this?' he whispers in your ear. Answer? God knows and it has been dealt with in the gospel. *There is therefore now no condemnation to them which are in Christ Jesus, who walk not after the flesh, but after the Spirit* (Romans 8:1). He can cause irrational panic as he did for David: *David said in his heart, I shall now perish one day by the hand of Saul*

(1 Samuel 27:1). Whatever, we need to grow in Christian discernment and we need to learn to recognise these flaming darts of the wicked one. We need to learn to use our God-given shield of faith (6:16). And do remember, it is only in a spiritually dry heart and life that Satan's fires can take hold.

(22)

The Devil's Doubts
(Ephesians 6:10-20)

The Roman shields for size would have been very much like those our modern-day police use but made of leather and very heavy. They would be used in grim situations to fend off hostile forces. They would catch and quench fiery arrows before they could ignite a fierce blaze. But the best way to have used them would have been in a company, shoulder to shoulder with other soldiers. It could have been in defence or attack. One of the devil's choice schemes (6:11) is, of course, to divide. He is likened to a roaring lion: *Be sober, be vigilant; because your adversary the devil, as a roaring lion, walketh about, seeking whom he may devour* (1 Peter 5:8). He is also like a ravening wolf, who likes to pick off individual stragglers—the weak or wounded, or those who have strayed. This was a strategy of Moab in the Old Testament, picking off the stragglers, the slow, the weary. This is why we need Christian fellowship, why we need to stay close to one another, because a united shield gives more protection, with security for the weak and wounded as well as the strong. This piece of our armour is of the utmost importance. It is a duty, yes, even more than a duty for all of us. Each one of us must be in our God-given place. That is of much importance. If King David had been in front of his troops, fighting alongside them, he would perhaps never have laid eyes on

Bathsheba. Are you in your God-appointed place? Are you in the Lord's battle and fighting—not your own little war, but fighting for God's cause? If you're out on your own you are in danger of being picked off by the enemy.

Also, it takes some effort to use the shield of faith. It must in faith be set before you, holding up the promises of God, but to do so they must be read and learned. The more saturated with the word of God you are, the better equipped you will be to deflect Satan's attacks. Study the temptations of your Master. See how he dealt with the enemy, answering each onslaught with the word of God, destroying his lies with truth and refuting his suggestions with divine wisdom.

The apostle Paul believed God: *But after long abstinence Paul stood forth in the midst of them and said, 'Sirs, ye should have hearkened unto me and not have loosed from Crete and to have gained this harm and loss. And now I exhort you to be of good cheer: for there shall be no loss of any man's life among you, but of the ship. For there stood by me this night the angel of God, whose I am and whom I serve, Saying, "Fear not, Paul; thou must be brought before Caesar: and, lo, God hath given thee all them that sail with thee." Wherefore, sirs, be of good cheer: for I believe God, that it shall be even as it was told me'* (Acts 27:21-25). He trusted God in a most perilous situation and God delivered him. There was nothing the devil could do to stop Paul from getting to Rome. How does he know this? Because God had already told him: *The night following the Lord stood by him and said, 'Be of good cheer, Paul: for as thou hast testified of me in Jerusalem, so must thou bear witness also at Rome'* (Acts 23:11). God does not change his mind. The issues are only confused when we fail to trust or mistrust God. His word is always good. Use the shield of faith.

The devil often oversteps himself. You must be aware that he fires all sorts of flaming darts at us, some making us doubt or even fear. But be encouraged, if his flaming darts are being fired at you it's because you are going on with the Lord. The devil would not be troubled with you otherwise (1 Peter 4:12). Of the ten virgins in Matthew 25, there were five who were ready (they were the Lord's, that's why) and five who were not. But read it again: *They all slumbered and slept* (Matthew 25:5). Are you awake, Christian? Are you not aware that *it is high time to awake out of sleep: for now is our salvation nearer than when we believed* (Romans 13:11)? When the flaming darts start to come at you the tendency is to run or to change direction. The need is to stand! And *to stand firm* (6:13).

(23)

The Devil's Designs (1)
(Ephesians 6:18)

With the shield of faith you are equipped to deal with, to quench, every flaming dart the devil throws at you—not just some, but all of them. You do well to also remember that in the noise and heat of the battle, no matter how fierce it becomes, you are never out of the sight of the Commander-in-Chief. He is not just watching you but praying for you unceasingly (Luke 22:31-32). He is always dynamically present with you. To utilise the shield of faith is to believe that with all your heart. One of the attacks of the enemy is to get you to doubt it; to believe because he is attacking you that God has left you and doesn't care. But this is not true, even if at times you feel it. It is the objective truth of God's written word. He has written down just in case you would forget: *I will never leave thee, nor forsake thee* (Hebrews 13:5) and, *If God be for us, who can be against us? He that spared not his own Son, but delivered him up for us all, how shall he not with him also freely give us all things? Who shall lay any thing to the charge of God's elect? It is God that justifieth. Who is he that condemneth? It is Christ that died, yea rather, that is risen again, who is even at the right hand of God, who also maketh intercession for us* (Romans 8:31-34). The devilish insinuation that God is not with you is a fierce lie from the very pit of hell. This is especially so when you are in trouble of your own making and have sinned, blundered, or failed in some way. He will suggest that God has now cast you off. This is where your shield comes in and must be employed. In faith you affirm— shout it out from the rooftops if needs be—God is good! God is loving! God is caring! God is compassionate! And his call is always that you turn to him in faith from whatever storm you may be facing and find refuge in him.

The thing we so often forget is that God is ever seeking us. Back in the garden of Eden, it was God who went seeking our parents. They were frightened, terrified, in hiding, but he still wanted them and went in search of them in love. So, tell me who is it that makes you feel rejected, useless, finished, or who casts us into depression? Yes, the devil, the enemy of your soul, the one who hates your Saviour and hates you because you love him. Some of his flaming darts are slow burners rather than fierce blazers. The devil's design is to cause long-term dis-ease. But however long it may take we pray in faith and wait on the Lord. He will come and he will deliver. This dis-ease, is designed to cause dis-peace. You've lost the *sense* of peace—but remember, losing the sense of something and losing the thing itself are two different things. You may flay yourself in rebuke, in shame, in agony, but this is not from God. This is not how he deals with his children. If something is wrong he may tell us firmly, but he shows us in order to correct us: *And if in any thing ye be otherwise minded, God shall reveal even this unto you* (Philippians 3:15). He will by his grace enable you to put it right. Be at peace, child of God, for his thoughts towards you are thoughts of peace: *For I know the thoughts that I think toward you, saith the Lord, thoughts of peace and not of evil, to give you an expected end* (Jeremiah 29:11). But Satan doesn't like peace. He is the disturber of such and that's why you and I need the shield of faith; why we need to go on as we started, in faith, believing. The enemy would have you to believe he is strong. He is not. But God is and he is our strength. Our lives are hidden in him so they are untouchable (Colossians 3:3). When we begin to grasp that God has provided for us his complete armour, we begin to understand what king David meant when he spoke of God providing a table of refreshment in the presence of his enemies. He has provided this for us also.

(24)

The Devil's Designs (2)
(Ephesians 6:10-20)

God has provided us with the helmet of salvation (6:17). This salvation is a present one. It saves and it keeps us safe, protecting us from a fatal blow to the head which would be the end of us. You will notice that all the parts of God's armour are defensive bar one. They are designed to protect us, not from suffering, but from sin that could be the end of us. It becomes clear that a large part of this warfare is to do with our minds and there is a lot of hard and clear thinking to be done. In other words, we have to keep our heads. God's salvation is our sure hope, the same hope that keeps our minds: *But let us, who are of the day, be sober, putting on the breastplate of faith and love; and for an helmet, the hope of salvation* (1 Thessalonians 5:8). And we are persuaded that we are, in this salvation, eternally secure, so that *neither by the blood of goats and calves, but by his [Jesus'] own blood he entered in once into the holy place, having obtained eternal redemption for us* (Hebrews 9:12). This is our irreversible, guaranteed hope. In our putting on the helmet of salvation (6:17) we are attuning to a biblical mindset, believing that salvation has dealt with our past, present and future sins. Therefore, we are able to rejoice in the midst of trials and tribulations (James 1:2; Romans 5:1-5). We can think clearly, calmly, rationally and expectantly in regard to the whole of life and its experiences. In other words we engage in right thinking. This is a repeated emphasis in the New Testament teaching that we should use our minds to think biblically and not in terms of the world's mindset (Romans 12:1f; Colossians 3:1f; Philippians 4:7f; 1 Peter 1:13). Think of all the Bible's references to the mind and to our thought-life. Isn't this how the devil attacks us, when in times of mental tiredness he seeks to lead us into confused thinking and thus discourage and even depress us?

The enemy's objective is to take our minds off God or to lead to wrong thoughts about God. He seeks to deceive and lead us astray by any means at his disposal, thus either hindering us or restricting our service for God. One of his schemes is to lead us into an obsession with some aspect of our faith. It is right and proper that we have a concern for people and for the church, but when it becomes excessive it is obsessive (2 Corinthians 2:12f; 7:5). It may be some aspect of the truth, about church government, or eschatology or any other Christian doctrine. We can very easily be obsessive about such things to the point of it being destructive to ourselves and others. The late Dr Martyn Lloyd-Jones used to say frequently that the Christian life was always a matter of balance, a healthy balance. Is there some aspect of the Christian life that is an obsession with you, leading you into conflict with others and spoiling your joy and your witness? Nobody, not even the spiritually strong and mature are immune to the subtle, disturbing assaults on the mind initiated by the devil, the enemy of our souls. He can make the most innocent comments register as clear criticism, accusation or a rejection of yourself that was never intended. That such thoughts come to us in a total and sweeping way and begin to cause destruction, dissension and division ought to tell you something of their origin. The helmet of salvation is a necessity (6:17).

(25)

The Battle for the Mind
(Ephesians 6:10-20)

The great battle of every generation, but particularly the present one, is for the minds of men and women. The enemy with his hosts operates in the intellectual, philosophical, theological and ideological arenas through the houses of learning—universities, colleges, the entire education system—seeking to poison the minds of our children and youth. They operate through the media and all of its outlets: advertising, soap operas, industry. There are no no-go areas for the enemy. We are fighting them on every level; and now the internet also, where anyone can freely and almost without hindrance propagate their favourite cause. The devil knows how to use a computer too. He puts relentless pressure on the minds of our young people in particular. The same evil genius was seen in the Nazi propaganda machine. It worked on the premise that if you said it often enough it would be believed. Thus we are bombarded with the lie of evolution, with immoral, anti-God and anti-biblical propaganda. The advertising machinery is a process of conditioning that's aimed at people's feelings rather than encouraging rational thought. This way people become 'feelings' oriented. People are moved by impulse or inclination rather than thought and fact. The advertising industry is an evil business. It affects Christians as well as the world, so that for many life has become experience-centred, dominated by passions and lusts, awakened by the images placed before us. It is, for this reason, Holy Scripture tells us we need to be renewed in our minds, not once, but constantly, daily: *And be not conformed to this world: but be ye transformed by the renewing of your mind, that ye may prove what is that good and acceptable and perfect, will of God* (Romans 12:2). Our minds need to be saturated with Scripture, so that we learn to think biblically at every turn in our lives. But sadly these are days in the Western church when such thinking is seriously lacking. Christians are not reading as they should and therefore they are not thinking as they ought.

This leads to a lack of sound doctrine and an absence of biblical patterns of behaviour. There are far too many who haven't thought through their faith and are unwilling to do so. Enter many a church in our land today and you'll find professing Christians who cannot state clearly what they believe, nor the grounds for it. Ask the person next to you, 'What is the gospel of which you speak?' The answers will vary and will be mostly wrong if you get an answer at all. So, what is the gospel then? That *Christ died for the ungodly* (Romans 5:6); that *Christ died for our sins according to the scriptures and that he was buried and that he rose again the third day according to the scriptures* (1 Corinthians 15:3-4). That's the gospel. Tragically, by and large, this is not the answer you will get, just their own limited experience or church tradition. The Bible warns of end-time delusions and lies: *Now the Spirit speaketh expressly, that in the latter times some shall depart from the faith, giving heed to seducing spirits and doctrines of devils; speaking lies* (1 Timothy 4:1-2); and, *for this cause, God shall send them strong delusion, that they should believe a lie* (2 Thessalonians 2:11). It's very easy to see how people can be led into all sorts of delusions and lies when people have surrendered in the battle for the mind. If we are losing this battle in the church how can we possibly expect to win it out there in the world; because unless we get the minds of the masses of unbelievers we will have very little effect upon them. So, the headgear, the helmet of salvation, is an indispensable piece of God's armour, to be put on each day.

(26)

The Sword of the Spirit
(Ephesians 6:10-20)

The only offensive weapon we have in this armour is the sword of the Spirit (6:17b), but notice: it is the sword *of the Spirit*—the Spirit's sword—and is therefore invincible. The Christian's warfare has to do with the mind, thinking, but with a Bible in hand: *I beseech you, therefore, brethren, by the mercies of God, that ye present your bodies a living sacrifice, holy, acceptable unto God, which is your reasonable service. And be not conformed to this world: but be ye transformed by the renewing of your mind, that ye may prove what is that good and acceptable and perfect will of God* (Romans 12:1-2). This is the means that the Holy Spirit uses and particularly when the word of God is preached. The undiluted word of God is the deadly scythe to cut down the enemies of God and his people. It is powerful and revealing: *I am not ashamed of the gospel of Christ: for it is the power of God unto salvation to every one that believeth; to the Jew first and also to the Greek. For therein is the righteousness of God revealed from faith to faith: as it is written, The just shall live by faith* (Romans 1:16-17). Since Christ is in it, it produces faith that leads to salvation: *Faith cometh by hearing and hearing by the word of God* (Romans 10:17). By it we taste the heavenly world (Hebrews

6:5). It is the Christian's weapon before which the demons flee (6:12). The truth is our belt (6:14); the gospel is our righteousness (6:v14b); peace tranquilizes the mind (6:15); and the shield protects us from the father of lies (6:16). The sword of the Spirit is the word of God and is our principle means of grace. What does grace mean? It is an attribute of God, his attitude of favour towards undeserving sinners. Grace is the power by which the sinner is saved and delivered from the bondage of sin and corruption. It is by grace we are regenerated, sanctified and made pleasing to God. Grace is a spiritual blessing and virtue bestowed by God. And how is it bestowed? By the preaching of God's word.

The Scriptures bring us to a conscious faith, but then there are what we would call the wider means, that of good Christian reading and of godly conversation with other saints—fellowship in other words. Fellowship is so misunderstood these days. It is not conversing about the week's work, or our favourite sports team or activities. It is conversing with and sharing the things of God with other believers. This is a means of edification, strengthening our faith. Some would include prayer, or one could go wider still and include *all* things—*And we know that all things work together for good to them that love God, to them who are the called according to his purpose* (Romans 8:28)—the temptations we face, the lures of the world, the fight with the flesh and all our sufferings and afflictions. To be sure God uses all these for our growth in grace: *And not only so, but we glory in tribulations also: knowing that tribulation worketh patience; and patience, experience; and experience, hope and hope maketh not ashamed; because the love of God is shed abroad in our hearts by the Holy Ghost which is given unto us* (Romans 5:3-5). In Reformed theology, however, we see the preaching of God's word as being the main means, the principal means of grace. It is by this means we are called by God to be Christians. It is by this means we receive the knowledge of Christ. And this without the sacraments, for they are added to the word. They are signs and seals of the promise of God. But it is the word that is primary and that explains the sacraments. It is the word that is indispensable. We can live without the sacraments, but not the word: *But he answered and said, It is written, man shall not live by bread alone, but by every word that proceedeth out of the mouth of God* (Matthew 4:4). It is the word that works faith, sustains our spiritual life and explains the sacraments. Without the word of God, the sword of the Spirit, the sacraments would be meaningless.

(27)

The Provision of Scripture
(Ephesians 6:10-20)

The sword here is the word of God (6:19), or the Bible, the Holy Scriptures. They are referred to as holy because they come from the God who is holy, thrice holy, utterly holy. The context is that of stance, making a stand against the enemy of God, of the church and of our own souls. The stance is not so much of standing still, but rather that of going forward against the enemy. It is in understanding this that we begin to realise the lengths the devil will go to in order to remove the word of God from us. He tries to cast doubts upon our minds, to damage our confidence in what God has spoken. Remember his words to Eve, 'Did God actually say (Genesis 3:1)?' That is still his insinuation today. He will use the doubt-ridden questioning of the higher critics and academia's persistent denials of the historic record of God's work of creation (Genesis 1-2). A multiplicity of Bible translations has caused much confusion amongst God's people—and this is not an attack on a good modern translation of the Bible.

There are also the errors and extremes of both the Charismatic and Pentecostal movements with the tendency to believe they have the Holy Spirit so the Bible is not quite so necessary, as well as accepting further so-called extra-biblical revelations. Claims have been made time and again that have been proved to be false, even contradicting the Bible. Let us be absolutely clear: the Holy Spirit never has, nor ever will, contradict his own God-breathed word (2 Timothy 3:16). The Holy Spirit speaks by this word. The summons of the Holy Spirit to the church, the people of God is to hear the word of God, the Holy Scriptures, read and preached. This is his provision for us and it is inspired and infallible—*All Scripture is breathed out by God and profitable for teaching, for reproof, for correction and for training in righteousness, that the man of God may be complete, equipped for every good work* (2 Timothy 3:16-17). Its preservation down the ages is truly remarkable.

The Bible is the truth about God himself, the only trustworthy revelation of the true and living God. Furthermore, it is a true revelation of ourselves, what we are truly like—not good, but deceitful, wicked, vile and in desperate need of the salvation Scripture declares to us through the Son of God. It is trustworthy in every detail: *Knowing this first, that no prophecy of the scripture is of any private interpretation. For the prophecy came not in old time by the will of man: but holy men of God spake as they were moved by the Holy Ghost* (2 Peter 1:20-21). It is a sure word of testimony, dependable because it comes to us from God. It is sharper than any sword: *For the word of God is quick and powerful and sharper than any two-edged sword, piercing even to the dividing asunder of soul and spirit and of the joints and marrow and is a discerner of the thoughts and intents of the heart* (Hebrews 4:12). It is to be used in all the work of God's salvation. It is this self-same word that the Holy Spirit uses to bring people to a conviction of their sinful state and condition before almighty God: *And when he is come, he will reprove the world of sin and of righteousness and of judgment: Of sin, because they believe not on me; Of righteousness, because I go to my Father and ye see me no more; Of judgment, because the prince of this world is judged* (John 16:8-11). It is through the sword of the Spirit that we are brought to a conscious, living faith: *So then faith cometh by hearing and hearing by the word of God* (Romans 10:17). *Who are kept by the power of God through faith unto salvation ready to be revealed in the last time* (1 Peter 1:5). How? By the living word of God. It is by this word we are sanctified and equipped for every good work that God has for us. How we should reverence our Bibles, counting them as precious; and especially so in these days of terrible apostasy and confusion. One of the Puritans on one occasion cried to God, 'Take away our children, our homes, our jobs, but please don't take your word away from us,' for without the word of God we would perish.

(28)

The Preaching of Scripture
(Ephesians 6:10-20)

There is an emphasis here on the provision of Scripture as a means of grace, but in particular, the preaching of those scriptures. This is the primary means of grace. The Christian's warfare is not just about having the sword of the Spirit, the word of God, but wielding that sword. It is for this reason that the apostle Paul asks for prayer as he himself wields the sword in the proclamation of the word (6:19), that he may be given utterance to boldly preach the word of God. This is the church's most vital weapon in her missionary endeavours: *For after that in the wisdom of God the world by wisdom knew not God, it pleased God by the foolishness of preaching to save them that believe* (1 Corinthians 1:21). And: *How then shall they call on him in whom they have not believed? and how shall they believe in him of whom they have not heard? and how shall they hear without a preacher?* (Romans 10:14)? It is not a matter of human eloquence, competence, or personality, but the Holy Spirit empowering the preaching of the word and applying it to the hearts of the hearers. Of course, there is no benefit if people do not hear and hear in faith (Hebrews 4:2), but it is the preaching of the word that brings conviction, that converts people (John 16:8-9). It is the Holy Spirit in conjunction with the word of God that leads us into the truth (John 14:25-26). He is our God-given librarian, remembrancer, bringing to mind the necessary truth as we most need it, in every circumstance and on all occasions. Whether it be the pulpit, the Sunday School, the Bible class, at home, in personal testimony, or in public street preaching, he affirms, assures and watches over his word to perform it (Jeremiah 1:12). God has promised and declared that it, his word, will accomplish his divine purpose in sending it forth: *For as the rain cometh down and the snow from heaven and returneth not thither, but watereth the earth and maketh it bring forth and bud, that it may give seed to the sower and bread to the eater: So shall my word be that goeth forth out of my mouth: it shall not return unto me void, but it shall accomplish that which I please and it shall prosper in the thing whereto I sent it* (Isaiah 55:10-11).

It is therefore vital that we handle the scriptures properly, correctly: *Of these things put them in remembrance, charging them before the Lord that they strive not about words to no profit, but to the subverting of the hearers. Study to shew thyself approved unto God, a workman that needeth not to be ashamed, rightly dividing the word of truth* (2 Timothy 2:14-15). We handle the scriptures with openness and honesty, not with a show of cleverness: *For Christ sent me not to baptize, but to preach the gospel: not with wisdom of words, lest the cross of Christ should be made of none effect"* (1 Corinthians 1:17). *And I, brethren, when I came to you, came not with excellency of speech or of wisdom, declaring unto you the testimony of God. For I determined not to know any thing among you, save Jesus Christ and him crucified. And I was with you in weakness and in fear and in much trembling. And my speech and my preaching was not with enticing words of man's wisdom, but in demonstration of the Spirit and of power: That your faith should not stand in the wisdom of men, but in the power of God* (1 Corinthians 2:1-5). In confidence we can take up the sword of the Spirit, knowing that he can make use of it as he only can, even with much power unto salvation. And that confidence comes more and more as we study and get to know our Bibles more accurately, thoroughly and comprehensively.

As we come to an end of this note take the time to read and meditate on Joshua 1:1-9, not forgetting of course prayer (6:18). It is said that the best form of defence is to attack. That way we keep the devil on the ropes, reeling even, with a constant barrage of effective thunderbolts from the word by prayer. When Jesus was being tempted in the desert by Satan it is almost as though he is baiting the devil. 'Go on. Have another go.' He has such confidence in the word of God and is ready to answer and defeat every argument thrown at him. 'It is written. It is written.' Never mind the 'I think' or 'I feel.' IT IS WRITTEN!

(29)

The Warrior's Praying
(Ephesians 6:18)

There are some who would think of this matter of prayer as an add-on rather than a piece of the armour of God: *Praying always with all prayer and supplication in the Spirit and watching thereunto with all perseverance and supplication for all saints* (Ephesians 6:18). However, I would ask, how is the armour to be put on, but by prayer? Each and every piece of the armour needs to be put on prayerfully in order for it to be effective. It is the way to bring heaven to our souls, to fetch the grace we need to fight the good fight of faith. The apostle seems to link three things together here—the word of God, the Spirit of God and the Spirit's constraint to pray at all times. The Spirit's influence is needed for freedom of utterance (6:19) and for clarity and liberty of mind and speech to make the gospel known (6:19). Prayer is the first response in this warfare. When faced with the threat of opposition Daniel simply carried on as was his custom: *Now when Daniel knew that the writing was signed, he went into his house; and his windows being open in his chamber toward Jerusalem, he kneeled upon his knees three times a day and prayed and gave thanks before his God, as he did aforetime* (Daniel 6:10). This should always be the norm for our churches and individual Christians, if for no other reason than that we are on a war footing all the time. Prayer ought to be the heart and life of the Christian church. The need is not for movements, for para-church organisations, for missions or anything else. The raising of such societies is usually an indication that the church herself is not doing what she ought to be doing, praying.

Remember what it is we are dealing with here, an enemy, the devil, called Satan. *Finally, my brethren, be strong in the Lord and in the power of his might. Put on the whole armour of God, that ye may be able to stand against the wiles of the devil. For we wrestle not against flesh and blood, but against principalities, against powers, against the rulers of the darkness of this world, against spiritual wickedness in high places* (Ephesians 6:10-12). We are constantly warring against his evil schemes and so need to be *praying always* (6:18). Perhaps we need more often to examine our commitment to the life and work of our local fellowship. That surely is where this battle is won or lost, especially the prayer meeting. As one renowned preacher put it, *The prayer meeting is the engine room of the church;* not special movements or occasions, but regularly, habitually, *praying always* (6:18). The word *always* (6:18) is sometimes misunderstood. It means just this: praying regularly, habitually. There are times when we need to be listening to sermons, or concentrating on doing our jobs. Sometimes we can be over-busy to the point where prayer gets pushed out altogether. I recall a minister once who, while visiting a fellow minister's home, was told by the minister's wife that her husband had something to confess. Expecting to hear of yet another case of adultery, the visiting minister was surprised to hear his host tell him that he hadn't prayed in over a year—and yet he was the minister of a large church. You see, you can do church, you can preach and you can build up a congregation with natural gifts, but if it is not done in dependence upon Christ what is it worth? *Now if any man build upon this foundation gold, silver, precious stones, wood, hay, stubble; Every man's work shall be made manifest: for the day shall declare it, because it shall be revealed by fire; and the fire shall try every man's work of what sort it is. If any man's work abide which he hath built thereupon, he shall receive a reward. If any man's work shall be burned, he shall suffer loss: but he himself shall be saved; yet so as by fire* (1 Corinthians 3:12-15). *Praying always* (6:18) means living a life that keeps walking with God, sensitive to his counsel. It is being engaged in a natural relationship talking to God in and about everything.

(30)

The Conflict of Prayer
(Ephesians 6:18)

There are many aspects to prayer: worship, adoration, praise, thanksgiving and intercession, but there are two things that prayer most certainly is not. It is not preaching and it is not for the correcting of others. I have heard people using prayer to both these ends. This is a great evil and must not be tolerated. But prayer is warfare. It could be said that this is the very epicentre of the battle, where it is won and lost. Our praying should be uttered in a way that all can understand and all can say a whole-hearted amen to at the close. (This, of course, excludes what people call praying in tongues, a spiritual gift now extinct). If we are taking part in a prayer meeting we should stand and speak clearly and loudly so that all can hear what is said. The early church gave itself to prayer and to the ministry of the word (Acts 6:1ff). If any of them were persecuted they would pray for them. When they prayed, things happened: society was shaken, prison walls were breached and lives were changed. In the Old Testament we have the example of the battle ebbing and flowing in direct proportion to the support given as Moses prayed (Exodus 17:8-13). This surely emphasises the importance of our attendance at the church prayer meeting. The Lord Jesus sees the needs of the people and he bids his disciples pray: *This kind can come forth by nothing, but by prayer and fasting* (Mark 9:29). Whatever the need or the situation we are instructed to take it to the Lord in prayer. We are always on a war footing and so our eyes and hearts need to be focused upon the Captain of our salvation.

We have this privilege, so we go to him and wait upon him in confidence. But we do so prepared to obey his orders whatever they may be. We are told here to pray *with all prayer and supplication* (6:18). *All prayer* means with all kinds of prayers. It doesn't always have to be formal, but simply speaking to God naturally as we go through our day. This is how our relationship, our friendship, with the Lord is established and maintained in freshness. It is vital. This is the Christian's life. Where there is no prayer there is no life. We can be on the move, maybe walking or driving, in any sort of posture, and very simply chat to God as we go about our daily chores. *Supplication* is getting down to specifics; praying about world affairs; the needs of people near and far; individuals in our own families; the church and its ministry; the needs of missionaries that we have a particular responsibility for;   and others the world over. We must inform ourselves in order to pray effectively. If we are praying about world affairs we need to make it our business to know about world affairs. There is no place in this Christian warfare for cosy, self-centered isolation. All the Lord's people are in this fight together,. Prayer is work. It is hard work and it takes effort. We need to remain alert. It is so easy to fall asleep at the wheel. Satan would rather rock you to sleep than come at you in a direct confrontational way. You know the penalty a soldier pays for falling asleep on active duty—the firing squad: *Praying always with all prayer and supplication in the Spirit and watching thereunto with all perseverance and supplication for all saints (Ephesians 6:18).*

(31)

The Conflict is a Spiritual One
(Ephesians 6:18)

We are thus instructed, *Praying always with all prayer and supplication in the Spirit* (6:18)—that is, with the help of the third Person of the Holy Trinity, the Holy Spirit. *Likewise the Spirit also helpeth our infirmities: for we know not what we should pray for as we ought: but the Spirit itself maketh intercession for us with groanings which cannot be uttered* (Romans 8:26). This has nothing to do with speaking in tongues. It is praying with a reliance upon the Holy Spirit to supply the necessary grace, help and energy to pray. Are there not times when we just don't know what to pray for? Prayer may be just simply a sigh. But the Holy Spirit knows how to present that sigh before God at the throne of grace fully knowing and expressing our state and our need. We are told here we must persevere in prayer, not because God is slow to answer or because he doesn't hear us. We just do not know the extent to which our prayers can set activity in motion in high places. It is in high and heavenly places where the real work of God is done and progresses. Think of the far-reaching effects of the prayers of former saints: *While I was speaking and praying and confessing my sin and the sin of my people Israel and presenting my supplication before the Lord my God for the holy mountain of my God; yea, while I was speaking in prayer, even the man Gabriel, whom I had seen in the vision at the beginning, being caused to fly swiftly, touched me about the time of the evening oblation* (Daniel 9:20-21). *Fear not, Daniel: for from the first day that thou didst set thine heart to understand, and to chasten thyself before thy God, thy words were heard and I am come for thy words* (Daniel 10:12). We are assured our prayers are heard. The value and significance of our prayers are seldom realised. Think of a small insignificant group of Christians gathered 'just to pray'. The prayers of the saints are the decrees of God beginning to work. It is nothing short of unbelief that caused the church prayer meetings in the West to diminish. It is the Holy Spirit's indwelling the Christian, without whom a person is not a Christian, who prompts and encourages us to pray. Without this divine Enabler, we would not know what to pray for. He is our inspiration, our energy, our power (Romans 8:26).

We see in the book of Revelation just how much the prayers of the saints on earth are so effective. There we see them being worked out on earth. We see the heavenly Lamb, the one who makes the throne a throne of grace, seated in the midst of his throne surrounded by his angelic helpers. *Seeing then that we have a great high priest, that is passed into the heavens, Jesus the Son of God, let us hold fast our profession...Let us, therefore, come boldly unto the throne of grace, that we may obtain mercy and find grace to help in time of need* (Hebrews 4:14, 16). It is there at the throne of grace we see our poor, feeble, stammering, limited prayers mingle with the incense of heaven, so reaching the throne of God in perfection, a sweet aroma in his nostrils. Beloved, if this is prayer in biblical terms then how important is our praying in its nature and its significance? We must see this aspect of our Christian warfare as the deepest secret and strongest power and engage. If praying is something that Christ ever lives to do (Hebrews 7:25), it must be important. It must be worth doing—daily, hourly pleading our case before the presence of God. If God be for us, will he leave us alone to pray (Romans 8:31)? Never! If he has given us his Son, will he not give us all else we need for this great conflict that we've been called into (Romans 8:32)? And since we pray in his name, not our own, will he not give us those things which we ask for? He will indeed.

The End

Soldiers Wanted

God give us men...ribbed with the steel of Your Holy Spirit...men who will not flinch when the battle's fiercest...men who won't acquiesce, or compromise, or fade when the enemy rages. God give us men who can't be bought, bartered, or badgered by the enemy, men who will pay the price, make the sacrifice, stand the ground, and hold the torch high. God give us men obsessed with the principles true to your word, men stripped of self-seeking and a yen for security...men who will pay any price for freedom and go any lengths for truth. God give us men delivered from mediocrity, men with vision high, pride low, faith wide, love deep, and patience long...men who will dare to march to the drumbeat of a distant drummer, men who will not surrender principles of truth in order to accommodate their peers. God give us men more interested in scars than medals. More committed to conviction than convenience, men who will give their life for the eternal, instead of indulging their lives for a moment in time. Give us men who are fearless in the face of danger, calm in the midst of pressure, bold in the midst of opposition. God give us men who will pray earnestly, work long, preach clearly, and wait patiently. Give us men whose walk is by faith, behaviour is by principle, whose dreams are in heaven, and whose book is the Bible. God give us men who are equal to the task. Those are the men the church needs today.

The Growth Factor, Bob Moorehead

www.ingramcontent.com/pod-product-compliance
Lightning Source LLC
Chambersburg PA
CBHW061043050726
47592CB00004B/1577